Karl Craven

# COLUMBUS

## & THE OHIO STATE UNIVERSITY
## THEN & NOW

# COLUMBUS

## & THE OHIO STATE UNIVERSITY
## THEN & NOW

KATHY MAST KANE
& DOREEN UHAS SAUER

THUNDER BAY
P·R·E·S·S

San Diego, California

**Thunder Bay Press**
An imprint of the Baker & Taylor Publishing Group
10350 Barnes Canyon Road, San Diego, CA 92121
www.thunderbaybooks.com

Produced by Salamander Books,
an imprint of Anova Books Ltd.
10 Southcombe Street, London W14 0RA, UK

"Then and Now" is a registered trademark of Anova Books Ltd.

All notations of errors or omissions should be addressed to Thunder Bay Press,
Editorial Department, at the above address. All other correspondence (author
inquiries, permissions) concerning the content of this book should be addressed
to Salamander Books, 10 Southcombe Street, London W14 0RA, UK.

Library of Congress Cataloging-in-Publication Data

Kane, Kathy Mast.
  Columbus and the Ohio State University then & now / Kathy Mast Kane, Doreen Uhas Sauer.
    p. cm.
  ISBN-13: 978-1-60710-010-2
  ISBN-10: 1-60710-010-X
  1. Columbus (Ohio)--Pictorial works. 2. Ohio State University--Pictorial works. 3. Columbus
(Ohio)--History--Pictorial works. 4. Ohio State University--History--Pictorial works. 5. Repeat
photography--Ohio--Columbus. I. Sauer, Doreen Uhas. II. Title. III. Title: Columbus and Ohio
State University then and now.
  F499.C743K36 2009
  977.1'56--dc22
                        2009014777

1 2 3 4 5 13 12 11 10 09

Printed in China

## ACKNOWLEDGMENTS

The authors would like to acknowledge two individuals, both having recently passed away, who were
instrumental in helping others to realize the importance of preserving the "Then" of Columbus. Dr. Paul
Young, Architecture, and Dr. Henry Hunker, Geography, both of the Ohio State University, in addition to
serving on the Board of Columbus Landmarks Foundation in its early years, both generously shared their
appreciation of the past with the community. Paul Young, a founding member of Landmarks' Education
Committee, fostered a love of the city's architectural details to all who met him. When hearing someone
talk about his or her "new" discovery regarding Columbus history or architecture, Paul Young would react
with delight and enthusiasm, rejoicing in the excitement of another's observation. Henry Hunker's courses
on urban geography were expeditions into his personal and well-mapped research for scores of Columbus
citizens, not just college students. A bus trip narrated by Dr. Hunker was a much anticipated venture. Both
were passionate urban storytellers and architectural adventurers.

In addition, three of the many local historical groups also deserve to be recognized: the City of Columbus
Historic Preservation Office and the dedicated volunteers serving in the city's system of historic
commissions, the Columbus Historical Society, and the Columbus Landmarks Foundation. They, as
respectful and vigilant caretakers of the city, past and present, nurture the "Now" of Columbus.

## PICTURE CREDITS

The publisher wishes to thank the following for kindly supplying the photographs that appear in this book:

"Then" photographs:
All "Then" images in the book were supplied courtesy of Columbus Metropolitan Library, Circulating
Visuals Collection, except for the following:
The Library of Congress: pages 32 inset (HABS OHIO,25-COLB,2-1), 38 (LC-D4-17365), 40 (LC-DIG-
det-4a23316), 50 (HABS OHIO,25-COLB,3-1), 76 main (LC-USZ62-75642), 136 inset (LC-D4-39071).
University District Organization: page 58.
Medical Heritage Center, the Ohio State University: page 112.
The Ohio Historical Society Archives: pages 14, 22, 60, 114, 116, 120, 122.
The Ohio State University Archives: pages 134, 136, 138, 140, 142.

"Now" photographs:
All "Now" images were taken by David Watts, except for pages 81, 115 (inset), 121, 135, 137 (main), 139,
141 and 143, which were taken by Kathy Mast Kane and Doreen Uhas Sauer.

# INTRODUCTION

Large tomes on the history of Columbus are available in public libraries, and each dark-covered book with brittle pages builds on the predecessors' research and adds eyewitness accounts or judgments about life in the city during the eighteenth, nineteenth, or early twentieth century.

There are also specialized narratives, almost "trade histories"—of the Diocese of Columbus, for instance—or a compilation of facts about the Columbus Public Schools up to 1924, or the Garden Club movement of 1913. Most are found in bookstores specializing in antique and used books, where one might also find memoirs of early Columbus childhoods. There is even history in tiny volumes of poems, like the one in which a genteel descendant of the city's founder wrote an ode to his office. When a book was published after World War I entitled *The Men Behind the Guns*, about how Columbus industrialists won World War I, it took another two decades before the women fired back with a book of their own, *We Too Built Columbus*.

There is also history in the landscapes, in the buildings, and in the stories of those who lived here and those who are constantly arriving.

The modern version of the multivolume history doesn't exist anymore. Perhaps the twentieth century got too complicated, too fast, or too expensive to reflect on and write about. The history of the twentieth-century city is found more in pieces—a monograph on a Works Progress Administration artist or the beginnings of a hospital, a 1928 master's thesis from an Ohio State sociology student, a now-lost historical society's bulletin that reprinted historical snippets, an artist's drawings enlivened with interviews, compendiums of newspaper columns from those salty sorts of 1940s newspapermen who covered Columbus from the crime scene to the all-night lunch counter, a biography of a war hero or a writer, a book of postcards, an Internet synopsis of a company's history, or a paperback of vignettes of places and people.

On the cover of an out-of-print children's book on Columbus's history, the founder of the city stands at the confluence of two rivers, shades his eyes, and looks to the 1950s skyline of the LeVeque Tower and the classical civic center. The picture is like the preferred ending to many early histories of Columbus, one in which we want to believe a city, in time, will improve like good wine. In this book, we have the advantage of being able to show both the "then" and the "now."

Though it must seem extraordinary for people to think that any part of Columbus dates back to the 1700s, it might be remembered that central Ohio was inhabited by the Wyandotte, Mingo, and Shawnee tribes; desired by the French who tromped around the flatlands, burying little markers for a nineteenth-century farmer to hit with a plow; claimed by the English who wanted anything the French desired; surveyed by new Americans who needed the land because they had no paychecks for the soldiers of the American Revolution; and ceded by Virginia to later become the first state carved from the Northwest Ordinance.

Franklinton, a small settlement on the west bank of the Scioto River in 1797, and its founders, especially Lucas Sullivant, promoted, bargained for, and created Columbus as a capital city, with its central location being perfect for a state capital. Franklinton, however, held out on being incorporated into Columbus until almost a hundred years later.

That Columbus exists at all is due to its peculiar role as a government center—for the city, for the county, for the state—and its location as a crossroads, whether for Native Americans who traveled north to south for fishing grounds on the Ohio River and hunting grounds in Upper Sandusky; or for the National Road, which opened the West to those hungry for inexpensive farmland; or for the railroads that cut diagonals across the state to link Ohio's big cities: Cleveland, Columbus, Dayton, and Cincinnati; or for the early airlines carrying mail, crossing the night sky guided by the LeVeque Tower beacon.

Before the Civil War, Columbus could be described as "the northernmost Southern city and the southernmost Northern city in Ohio." Though geographically north, Columbus attracted many Southerners. Franklinton's settlers (rich and poor) were from Virginia and Kentucky. In addition, New Englanders, freed slaves, Irish and Germans escaping from famine and political unrest, Pennsylvania farmers, and sons and daughters of prominent Eastern families arrived. Southern sympathizers, vehement abolitionists, and much of President Abraham Lincoln's cabinet and military leadership emerged from here.

Following the Civil War, the wealth of Columbus came from the coal, timber, and natural gas of southern Ohio, which fueled foundries, buggy makers, and shoe manufacturers. These industries drew in Italians, Greeks, Hungarians, and Croatians looking for work. But industry never ringed the downtown (and a present-day surprise to visitors is the intact neighborhoods nestled close in). The city's fortunes turned to banking, insurance, pharmaceuticals, and education. However, as late as the 1950s, the historic heart of Columbus's crossroad, the corner of Broad Street and High Street, was noted by linguists as a rare "geographic" and not imaginary isogloss, a demarcation between different syntax and pronunciation. If one were asked to pronounce the word "push," the speaker's birthplace in Columbus could be accurately judged by the linguist.

The "now" of Columbus may be best characterized by two men, both of whom had their adult accomplishments in early twentieth-century Columbus—one famous, one not.

George J. Karb was born in the 1850s and died in the 1930s. He was progressive, public-pleasing, and always cheerful about civic affairs. A councilman, a police commissioner, and a mayor who served several terms, Karb was a second-generation German who could speak in French or Welsh, or come out with a song, to please a crowd. His popular summary of the city, sometimes even seen in the national press, was "Good old Columbus town."

James Thurber, a timeless American humorist in an age that produced Hemingway and Faulkner, wrote in *My Life and Hard Times*, "In the early years of the nineteenth century, Columbus won out, as state capital, by only one vote over Lancaster, and ever since then has had the hallucination that it is being followed, a curious municipal state of mind which affects, in some way or other, all those who live there."

Curiously, the Columbus that was created to be a state capital (but was historically a small Ohio city compared to Cleveland and Cincinnati) has become the largest of the cities, the only one among the eight largest cities in Ohio that is still growing. It is a city that has long viewed itself as the bridesmaid but is now the bride. Unfettered of annexation issues that frustrated other cities' ambitions, progressively and conservatively liberal in politics, and rich in the resources of its diverse populations of newly arrived immigrants and students who settled there by way of the Ohio State University and six other universities, present-day Columbus remains "Good old Columbus town," a city given to an optimistic sense of can-do spirit.

In the 1880s, when this photo was taken, then-governor Rutherford B. Hayes rented a residence on East Broad Street. The four-towered Board of Trade Building—on the site of the venerable Buckeye House tavern—reflects the prosperity of small businesses; by 1910, the renamed Chamber of Commerce had 1,000 business members. Architect Elah Terrell chose a Richardson Romanesque front but miscalculated a construction technique used in the basement. The ceiling collapsed; two workers died. Left of the Board of Trade is the Hayden Bank, whose industrialist owner also owned foundries, 3,000 acres of coalfields, and the town of Haydenville. The fast-growing First Congregationalist Church (to the right of the Board of Trade) was already in its third building due to the popularity of its minister, Dr. Washington Gladden, founder of the Social Gospel movement, a pillar of the Progressive reform era. St. Joseph's Cathedral (far right) started as a church in 1866 but opened as the cathedral for the newly created Diocese of Columbus in 1872.

The Harrison Building (far left) and the Hayden Building next to it were early skyscrapers, built between the 1890s and early 1900s. These skyscrapers were the second generation of downtown buildings that replaced the pre–Civil War structures. Both buildings are being redeveloped, part of a popular revival of adaptive reuse of downtown buildings in the last decade, many for residential use. In 1969 part of the facade of the Chamber of Commerce Building collapsed onto the sidewalk in the early hours of the morning; no one was hurt. The building was quickly razed in order to construct the Rhodes State Office Tower (1974), named for Ohio's longest-serving governor, James Rhodes. At 629 feet high, the Rhodes Tower overshadows the oldest remaining building on Capitol Square, the former Hayden Bank (altered around 1920). Peregrine falcons nest on the ledge of the Rhodes Tower's forty-first floor; they have been viewed around the world by a Webcam that was installed in 1997.

Constructed in the 1890s and shown here in 1903, the Masonic Temple reflects the era when clubs and fraternal organizations were extremely popular, especially for men who wished to assume a mantel of civic leadership and further their business connections. The size of the Masonic Temple, and a major addition in the early twentieth century that doubled its size, suggests that the structure, with a large two-story auditorium and banquet room, a great number of smaller meeting spaces, a commodious kitchen, and many small, decorated chapel-like rooms, was a key meeting place. One important element of the addition was a classical four-columned projection, centered on the facade's upper story; it has since been removed.

In the late 1990s, after the Masons announced their decision to close their operation, a dramatic rally ensued to keep this prominent downtown building from being turned into a parking lot. The Ohio Preservation Alliance helped facilitate a sale to a group of investors only hours before all the furnishings and fixtures were to go on sale to the crowds who were waiting at the door in lines that snaked around the block. In 1996, the building's centennial year, the renovated Columbus Athenaeum opened its doors, having adapted the elaborately adorned theaters and meeting rooms, painted murals, rich wood-paneled walls, stenciled artwork, and marble lobby of the Masonic Temple for use as an elegant venue for special events. The Masonic Temple is listed in the National Register of Historic Places.

The Broad Street Bridge (to the left) was the fourth bridge to connect both sides of Columbus across the Scioto River at this site. Shown here circa 1906 (before the devastating 1913 flood that inundated Columbus's west side), both banks of the Scioto River were little more than rims to an open trench of industrial waste, sewage, and offal. Tenements and squalid living conditions can be seen on the east side of the river. A metal foundry stood at the site of the present city hall, within blocks of the statehouse. During the 1913 flood, all bridges south of Fifth Avenue, with the exception of an iron railroad bridge near the penitentiary on Spring Street, were destroyed. A radical urban facelift had been in the works since 1908, inspired by the City Beautiful movement of Chicago, and the flood gave Columbus the opportunity, from 1913 to World War II, to transform the riverfront into a classically inspired civic center.

After the 1913 flood, the fifth Broad Street Bridge was built in 1921. It was a classically inspired, seven-span concrete arch bridge designed in coordination with the new civic center buildings. When it was announced in the 1980s that the Broad Street Bridge would be replaced due to deterioration, debate ensued about the proposed design. The new bridge would set a design standard for the eventual replacement of other bridges. The Discovery Bridge, dedicated in 1992, is a five-span reinforced concrete design that complements the character of the civic center. The deteriorating Town Street Bridge, of a similar design, will be demolished but not rebuilt. The 1937 Main Street Bridge, a Federal Public Works project of Art Deco design (closed in 2002 and demolished) is being replaced with the nation's first inclined, single-rib tied arch bridge, only the fifth inclined arch superstructure in the world. The Scioto River Bridge Group was listed in the Columbus Register of Historic Properties, although none of them remain standing.

In 1839 the Ohio legislature called for the building of a statehouse in the Greek Revival style, to be completed in two years for $450,000. Sixty sets of plans were submitted and bitter political warring followed, often halting construction. When it opened in 1861, twenty-two years had passed and three times more money was spent—the statehouse could be called both a stunning, architecturally significant work (planned decades ahead of the U.S. Capitol in Washington) and a quintessential public works project. After

President William McKinley's assassination in 1901, Columbus memorialized the former Ohio governor with a sculpture of McKinley as he delivered his last address at the Pan-American Exposition. The statue was unveiled in 1906 by President Teddy Roosevelt's daughter, Alice. William McKinley's statue stands in front of the statehouse at the spot where he turned each day to wave to his wife Ida, who watched him from the window of their hotel room across the street.

Three major changes occurred over the course of the twentieth century. First, the "temple on the hill," as the statehouse was known, was joined by a controversial neighboring building in 1901 (now the Senate Building). Second, modernization dictated that an underground parking garage be built in the 1960s; all original or sizable trees on the grounds were lost. Third, Ohio's Capitol Square complex—the Ohio Statehouse, Senate Building, and Atrium—underwent a major restoration beginning in 1989. Rehabilitation of the Senate Building and the new Atrium space was completed in 1992, and the statehouse was restored by 1996. Treatments ranged from installation of state-of-the-art technology to reintroducing light to the rotunda's 1849 skylight of the great seal of Ohio. The statehouse is a National Historic Landmark, recognized for the purity of its Greek Revival architecture, and is also listed in the National Register of Historic Places and the Columbus Register of Historic Properties.

Columbus residents might remember the 1887 Old Federal Building as Columbus's second post office. Within twenty years of opening, the building's footprint was increased by 131 feet—the expansion was done so well that many cannot find where the new and the old join. With the addition, original Romanesque features were removed, and three arches and a matching entrance on Third Street were added to make the High Victorian Gothic building seen here. Columbus may be unique in that it has all of its old main post offices—often referred to as the Old Post Office, the Old Old Post Office, and the Old Old Old Post Office. The pioneer Deardurff log home of 1807 (see inset) is the Old Old Old Post Office on Gift Street (so named because the founder of Franklinton, Lucas Sullivant, made "gifts" of the lots to encourage settlement). Mail was brought from Chillicothe, Ohio, once a week on horseback, a trip of three days over uncharted terrain.

Columbus's Old Old Post Office is the headquarters for Bricker and Eckler, a prominent law firm founded in Columbus in 1945. The firm moved into the sensitively restored building in 1986, taking advantage of federal tax credits available for the rehabilitation of buildings listed in the National Register of Historic Places. When the post office moved out in 1934, the building sat nearly vacant and in deteriorated condition until the late 1970s. Inspired by Bricker and Eckler's vision for the building, the City of Columbus purchased it from the federal government in 1985. The restoration received the James B. Recchie Design Award from the Columbus Landmarks Foundation. The Old Old Old Post Office, the oldest log building in Columbus standing on its original site, is privately owned and is now threatened due to its deteriorating condition. The Old Post Office, now the Joseph P. Kinneary United States Courthouse, functioned as a post office from 1934 to 1969.

The Columbian Building (far left) was built between 1924 and 1926 to house the Columbian Savings and Loan Company. By 1942 the building was known as the Nitschke Building, taking the name of the family who owned the property even prior to the Columbian's founding. Nitschke Office Supply was a tenant in the building for many years thereafter. The Citizen Building (behind the lamppost) was built in 1917 by the architectural firm of Richards, McCarty, and Bulford, who created an ornate version of a neoclassical building; more floors were added in the 1960s. Gay Street in the early twentieth century housed small businesses, luncheonettes, dance academies, retail stores, banks, the B. F. Keith Theatre, and, at the corner of East Gay and High streets, the second Columbus Dispatch Building (1907), which replaced an earlier one destroyed by fire. The street is a zoo of stone creatures—griffins, owls, bees, eagles—as symbolic representations of original businesses.

This block of East Gay Street is listed in the National Register of Historic Places. It is distinguished by the sense of historical continuity gained from the uninterrupted rhythm and common setback of facades, and by its variety of architectural styles and details. Once home to many offices and banks, today the street is experiencing a revival. Mixed in with the traditional uses are restaurants, a hotel, and residential condominiums. The street recently experienced an additional makeover between High Street and Grant Avenue when two-way traffic was returned to the street in the interest of making it a more pedestrian-friendly corridor. In June 1984, a hundred-ton concrete cornice fell from the Nitschke Building. Former state senator Ben Espy, then a Columbus city councilman, and two other pedestrians were severely injured when hit by debris. In response to the accident, the Columbus City Council mandated in 1985 that downtown buildings with three or more stories would be required to submit proof of inspection of their cornices every five years.

In 1885 the famous Smith's European Hotel (and later café with an oyster bar) stood on the northeast corner of East Broad and North High streets. By 1900 Columbus was a combination urban center and hub of a large agricultural district. The Consolidated Street Railway operated all but one street railroad throughout the city by 1885; fourteen different railroad lines entered the city, linking Columbus to other cities. Modern electric arches, sponsored by business associations, had first appeared for Columbus's hosting of the reunion of the Grand Army of Republic in 1888, which brought 40,000 visitors to the city; the arches then remained for use with streetcars' electric lines. (Columbus became known as "the Arch City" for its large number of electric arches.) Over time, the European Hotel would bear names of other owners, and it housed many different businesses over the decades. Two of the more famous were Roy's Jewelers (with its over-the-top electric signs) and the tucked-away Benny Klein's restaurant (with belly dancers).

The former home of the European Hotel lasted into the twenty-first century, though parts of it were almost unrecognizable from modern facelifts. Plans for the adaptive reuse of the building were shut down, however, when a massive billboard on the roof collapsed into the building. The newest development, called Broad and High, is a mixed-use project consisting of offices, residential condominiums, commercial storefronts, and the local NBC television affiliate. Office and commercial space is located in a new building that mimics the four-story redbrick European Hotel building. It is, however, unmistakably new with multimedia billboard advertising attached. The former Capital Trust Building at 8 East Broad has been adapted for residential condominium use, and is known as 8 on the Square; it overlooks Capitol Square. Arches, once found throughout Columbus, have been re-created farther north on High Street in the Short North Arts District.

From 1895 until 1923, forty different automakers were located in Columbus, including the Columbus Buggy Company (1870–1914), which used, at various times, a systematized assembly line, loans from C. D. Firestone, and good business sense. By the 1890s, the company employed more than 1,200 people and had annual sales of $2 million. In 1903 they produced their first electric car, and in 1904 they relocated to Dublin Avenue. By 1913 the Buggy Company was bankrupt due to the Model T's ascendancy, Firestone's death,

the 1913 flood, and Eddie Rickenbacker, who left the company to race for companies with more powerful cars. A second generation of automakers can be seen in both the Allen Motor Company (occupying the Dublin plant site from 1919 to 1922; see inset), which built colorful touring cars, and in the Ford Motor Company (opening in 1913), which had fully equipped sales and assembling departments and 350 employees on the site of the former Neil Park baseball field.

At the same time that the Columbus Buggy Company met its demise, the Ford Motor Company made an appearance in Columbus, and stayed until 1939. The former Ford Motor Company is now a bakery for the Kroger Company, which built an adjacent building in 1926, expanding into the former Ford plant. The buggy manufacturing plant and the Allen Motor Company were converted to urban lofts in 2004, appropriately named the Buggyworks. A second phase, the Firestone Lofts, includes residential lofts and commercial, office, and retail space in the adjacent building. Where autos once followed baseball, baseball will follow buggies. Both residential spaces are in the newly developed downtown neighborhood, the Arena District, a baseball's throw from the new Huntington Park, built for the Columbus Clippers minor league baseball team.

Twenty years after the 1913 flood, with a widened Scioto River and angled bridges to prevent future flood debris jams, the 1927 American Insurance Union Citadel (later known as the LeVeque Tower) commands the new face of the riverbank with a plume of steam. With a height of 555 feet 6 inches, it was designed to be exactly six inches taller than the Washington Monument. At its feet is the Columbus City Hall (1928). To the left is the Old Post Office (now the Joseph P. Kinneary United States Courthouse), which opened in 1934 with President Franklin D. Roosevelt in attendance. To the right, by the Broad Street Bridge, is the Ohio Departments of State Building (1933), a fourteen-story white Georgian marble structure with two large reflecting pools, exterior sculptures, and interior details of bronze, brass, stainless steel, and marble, plus decorative murals in fine Art Deco detailing—all relating to the history of Ohio. The western approach to the city was the result of the City Beautiful movement in Columbus.

Prominent and unifying in Columbus's civic center today is a complex of buildings that includes the Ohio Judicial Center (1933), Columbus City Hall (1928), the Old Central Police Station (1928), and the Joseph P. Kinneary United States Courthouse. On the west side of the river is the Center of Science and Industry. The development of this complex was inspired in part by a plan developed for the city in 1908. Although the 1908 plan was not adopted when prepared, catastrophic damage from the flood of 1913 made redevelopment a necessity. A new downtown emerged with the civic center, based on the widening of the river, replacement bridges, and construction of flood walls. The Scioto Mile, a public-private project that includes a landscaped promenade and centerpiece fountain, will both beautify and give access along the river corridor. It will connect the recently developed North Bank Park with the southern Bicentennial Park (1976), to be completed for the city's bicentennial in 2012.

Opened in 1928 and designed by Thomas Lamb (who also designed the Palace Theatre), the Ohio Theatre was built to be a movie palace—fanciful, otherworldly, and over the top. Behind a rather severe facade are Spanish Baroque three-story lobbies, lounges, and public spaces, which had tapestries, painted murals, pendulum lamps, and European furnishings and antiques. These served to prepare the filmgoer for the visual stimulation of the auditorium—3,000 seats, balconies, an enormous chandelier with flying horses, giant bare-breasted nymphs above the stage, gargoyles, classical women's faces, and Corinthian columns—all gilded, of course. To the left is Isaly's, a chain of family-owned dairies and restaurants. Isaly's started in Mansfield, Ohio, and expanded its milk business into ice cream, bread, and luncheonette service. By the 1930s, their commercial buildings used distinctive Art Deco vitro glass facades and interiors. Isaly's was known for its Klondike Bars, Skyscraper Cones, and chipped ham.

The Ohio Theatre, a National Historic Landmark, was saved from demolition in 1969 through private donations and the efforts of the newly formed Columbus Association of Performing Arts (CAPA), which purchased the renovated theater. All of the embellishments and many of the furnishings remain. The Ohio is the home of the Columbus Symphony Orchestra. To better adapt the original movie theater's conversion to live performances, the John and Dorothy Galbreath Pavilion was added to the east side of the building in 1984. The addition provided dressing rooms, public gathering, and rehearsal and office space. The pavilion was awarded the James B. Recchie Design Award by the Columbus Landmarks Foundation. To the west of the Ohio stands the extensively remodeled Art Moderne–style Beggs Building (built in 1928 and extended in 1991) and the Fifth Third Center (1998); to the east stand two triangular towers, the Capitol Square Office Building (1984) and the Hyatt on Capitol Square (1984).

For five decades, the landmark destination and most famous corner in Columbus was the Deshler Hotel. David Deshler, a carpenter from Pennsylvania, came to Columbus with his young wife, Betsy, and bought the corner lot in 1817 for his home. The price was $1,000, including a gold watch. Deshler's son William tore down the house in 1878 to build the Deshler Bank, and in 1912 William's son John announced plans for the Deshler Hotel. The Deshler-Wallick (leased to the Wallick brothers of New York) contained 400 guest rooms, ballrooms, restaurants with gold table service, and the famous Ionian Room. In 1927 rooms were added in the new AIU Building next door and were reached through an elegant "Venetian bridge." The flamboyant mayor of New York, Jimmy Walker, came to inaugurate the event. In the 1940s, it was renamed the Deshler-Hilton, then the Deshler-Cole, and by the 1960s it was the Beasley-Deshler. By this time, rumors of its demise were no longer greatly exaggerated.

The Deshler-Wallick Hotel was closed in 1968 and demolished the next year. The corner of Broad and High streets, one of the prime parcels of real estate in downtown Columbus, sat empty or underutilized as a parking lot until 1986, still owned in a series of trusts by descendants of the Deshler family who were spread out across the country. (Ironically, though the famous Deshler name left the corner after 174 years, the small diary that Betsy Deshler left before she died in her twenties has lived on as the best account of early life in Columbus). In 1986 the cornerstone for One Columbus was set, and the office tower is among the tallest buildings in the city; its major tenants include U.S. Bank. The Palace Theatre, adjacent to One Columbus, was acquired by the Columbus Association of Performing Arts in 1989. Katherine LeVeque, daughter-in-law of one of the partners who owned the LeVeque Lincoln Tower, saved the Palace Theatre from neglect and destruction when she personally directed its restoration and refurbishing.

The original Columbus City Hall, built in 1928, was designed by an unusual collaboration of architects, the Allied Architects Association of Columbus, which formed after the destructive 1913 flood to rebuild the river area as a neoclassical civic center. The low-profile, Ionic-columned limestone building, surrounded by green space, is a prominent feature of the classical grouping of buildings. The most famous and prominent statue of Christopher Columbus as public art in the city stands on the south side of city hall (see inset). The statue, which is twenty feet tall and weighs three and a half tons, was the work of the Italian sculptor Edorado Alfieri, and was a gift from the city of Genoa, Italy, to Columbus in 1955. The name "Columbus" was suggested for the new capital of Ohio—which emerged on the high side of the Scioto River in 1812—by pioneer Joseph Foos, himself a boatman who ferried people across the river.

City hall changed from a C-shaped building to a blocky O when a fourth side was added in 1936 and the central courtyard was enclosed in 1949. Inside, the building retains the original stylish trim that was popular in the 1920s. The second-floor city council chamber—decorated in Abyssinian-Egyptian, classical, and Art Deco motifs in colors of terra-cotta, gold, and azure—was restored in 1986. A curved stairway to the second floor is decorated with Roman fascia. In the foreground outside is the Battelle Riverfront Park, which includes a variety of mixed-motif memorials and sculptures—the Firemen's Eternal Flame Memorial, the Columbus Children's Fountain, a plaque for John Brickell's 1797 log cabin, a monument to Italian Americans in Columbus, and even (in the river) a full-scale replica of the *Santa Maria*, built for the 1992 celebration of the 500th anniversary of Christopher Columbus's arrival in the New World.

The *Columbus Dispatch*, "Ohio's Greatest Home Newspaper," has been a fixture in Columbus since 1871 and on this site since 1925; it outgrew or lost (by arson in retaliation for the paper's disclosures of city hall graft) its previous locations. Though the building's facade is essentially unchanged, the building was greatly expanded in the 1950s when the *Columbus Citizen* and *Ohio State Journal* merged as the *Citizen-Journal* and were published out of the same building. The Wolfe family has been associated for five generations with journalism, politics, and philanthropy in Columbus since Harry P. and Robert F. Wolfe, owners of the Wolfe Brothers Shoe Company and the *Ohio State Journal*, bought the *Dispatch* in 1905. The Wolfes also own WBNS-TV; the initials are said to stand for "Banks, News, Shoes"—historic Wolfe interests. The American Education Press Building (1931) on the right was designed by the prestigious Columbus architectural firm of Richards, McCarty, and Bulford, using an appropriate facade for a publishing house—each metal spandrel contained a cast-metal punctuation mark or letter of the alphabet.

Though the Columbus Dispatch Building is virtually unchanged on the exterior, complete with the signature neon sign on top, the recently installed "ticker-tape" electronic sign placed above the first floor has updated the building's facade. In 1956 the Columbus Dispatch Building was expanded to the rear, stretching the entire block between Third and Fourth streets. This addition has since been removed. The American Education Press Building (also known as the University Club Building) was demolished in 1990. The nationally distributed *My Weekly Reader* children's magazine was published by the American Education Press. The University Club, originally a private men's club, occupied the top floors from when the building opened until it was demolished.

Memorial Hall (left), the Kelley mansion (see inset), and the Christopher Inn (center) have an interlocking history. In 1906 the Franklin County Memorial Hall at 280 East Broad Street was dedicated to be an all-purpose auditorium, convention center, sports venue, and a memorial for the soldiers and sailors of Franklin County who died in the Civil War. By the time it was built, veterans of the Spanish-American War were also honored. From 1906 to 1946, luminaries like Enrico Caruso, Marian Anderson, Isadora Duncan, Sergey Rachmaninoff, and John Philip Sousa performed there. Memorial Hall, designed by Frank Packard, was built next door to Alfred Kelley's 1832 Greek Revival mansion. Kelley pledged his house as collateral on the New York Stock Exchange in order to save Ohio's reputation following the financial panic of 1837. Kelley's house became the Catholic Diocese's Cathedral School. The mansion was demolished in 1961 and was replaced by a fifteen-story circular motel-restaurant, the Christopher Inn.

By the 1950s, Memorial Hall was considered a white elephant. Voters defeated bond levies for its refurbishing because a new veterans' memorial was planned. In the 1970s, the hall was given a new purpose as the Center of Science and Industry (COSI), sharing space with the Franklin County Historical Society. The building was extensively remodeled with a contemporary glass facade in 1973–74. Twenty-five years later, the COSI facade was removed and Memorial Hall was restored for use as Franklin

County government offices. The original plaques and memorials were placed in the post–World War II Veterans' Memorial on West Broad Street. On the right is the State Employees Retirement System Building (2002). The stones from the demolished Kelley mansion were relocated several times for a planned rebuilding (and still lie in wait at Hale Farm and Village near Akron). The site of the Christopher Inn, which was demolished in 1988, is now occupied by a parking lot.

Built in the 1860s by railroad contractor and banker Benjamin Smith, the house still stands as a reminder of the many prestigious homes that stretched out East Broad Street in the nineteenth and early twentieth centuries. The most lavish expenditures were used both in construction and for interior details. Each of the "Philadelphia pressed bricks" used in the construction arrived at the site wrapped separately in paper. True to the risks of business in the Gilded Age, Smith's fortune vanished when he attempted to establish a rival to New York's Coney Island. The home was a governor's mansion for two Ohio governors, George Hoadley and Joseph Foraker. It was purchased in the 1880s to be a prestigious private men's club. This photograph dates from 1896.

The Columbus Club is a rare remnant of what was built as a mid-nineteenth-century single-family residence, which still stands on a prominent corner location downtown. Functioning as a private club since it first opened in 1887, this well-maintained building with its original iron fences and carriage house (now attached) at the rear is an elegant reminder of a bygone era.

Interior spaces of the Columbus Club were redesigned by Columbus's preeminent architect, Frank Packard, who had led the remaking of the civic center. Among the notable spaces is the Tiffany Room, an intimate Arts and Crafts–style dining room bedecked with rich wood paneling and stained-glass light fixtures from the Tiffany Studios.

This 1909 photo shows the sprawling gingerbread cottage at the corner of Sixth and State streets. Built by Dr. Francis Carter in the 1840s and designed by New York architect Richard Sheldon, the home was quaint and Gothic. St. Francis Hospital, built across the street by the same architect, was, by contrast, turreted and Gothic. Carter, who wanted to see Columbus become a medical center for the region, mortgaged (and lost) the house to the financially secure St. Francis Hospital. Ohio governor Salmon P. Chase bought the house in 1857 for his two daughters, one of whom was the strong-minded Kate Chase, who made the cottage a political hotbed in her efforts to promote her father as president of the United States. Instead he became secretary of the treasury under Abraham Lincoln. Later, industrialist Peter Hayden also lived there.

The Knights of Columbus bought the Carter house, took down most of it, and built an auditorium in 1924 on part of the lot, leaving a single room of the cottage attached. The auditorium was remodeled for the Byer and Bowman Advertising Agency in 1952, at which time the last room of the cottage was razed. The Knights of Columbus Building shown here was constructed in 1926 on another section of the original lots. The building was donated to the Salesians of St. John Bosco by the Knights of Columbus Council in 1968, for their use as the Salesian Inner City Boys Club. Facilities in the building included a swimming pool, bowling alley, gymnasium, and computer labs. Their role has expanded to serve more than 3,000 boys and girls at this center, particularly through after-school programs and summer camps. Their doors closed in 2008, ending programs for children's social development, special education, and the prevention of drug and alcohol abuse. The Salesian Society is currently utilizing the building as a residence for retired priests.

Columbus came to life partly due to a state penitentiary. The company that promoted the building of the new state capitol in 1812 agreed to provide two sites—one for the state capitol and another for a penitentiary. When the original penitentiary was quickly outgrown, a new site was donated in 1832 by Columbus businessmen eager to use the convict labor and desirous of jobs and a market for local goods; it was said that if a city could not attract a university, a prison was almost as good. Ohio's early model of the new "penitent" system of reforming criminals was based on the Auburn Prison in New York. For most of its 170-year history, the buildings inside the twenty-four-foot-high, 400-foot-long stone walls fascinated Columbus residents, who could tour the prison. Behind the Victorian facade were 1830s walls and the stories of Confederate captain John Hunt Morgan's escape, the incarceration of writers O. Henry and Chester Himes, the 1930 fire, the 1938 tornado, and "Old Sparky," the 1897 electric chair.

The penitentiary closed in 1984 and was sold to the City of Columbus in 1995. After much debate, the entire complex was demolished in 1998. The condominiums of Burnham Square and mixed-use office and retail space fill a portion of the former site; much is still waiting to be developed. A remnant arch of Union Station is the centerpiece of McFerson Commons Park. Located in the vicinity of the former penitentiary, the urban riverfront North Bank Park opened in 2005. It is an eleven-acre park that is also the gateway to downtown workers and an inviting amenity for the growing downtown residential population. Major features in the park include a glass pavilion for special events, an amphitheater, interpretive historical panels, and a fountain for children. Much of the park's stone was recycled from the penitentiary. The North Bank Park and Pavilion received the James B. Recchie Design Award from the Columbus Landmarks Foundation.

The site of the future Carnegie Library was a no-man's-land into the 1840s. The land on Seventh Street (later Grant Avenue) was cheap, out of town, and had a frog pond at its front door, making it economical for Noah Swayne, a Virginia lawyer, abolitionist, and new U.S. attorney for Ohio, to purchase it in 1840. He built a colonial-style home where present-day State Street ends. Six governors later lived in the house, and the mansion and the land were sold to the city for a new library in 1901. Columbus librarian John Pugh talked philanthropist and industrialist Andrew Carnegie into building a brick library at a time when Carnegie was moving out of the library business. When Pugh returned home, Columbus's movers and shakers told him they expected a marble library and demanded that he go back to ask for one. Amazingly, Carnegie agreed, choosing architect Randolph Ross of New York (who had designed almost two dozen previous Carnegie libraries) to oversee the design. This photo is from 1907, the same year the library was dedicated.

The original Carnegie Library was rehabilitated and expanded in 1989–91, more than tripling its space. The white marble rear addition complements the original 1907 building. The sensitive restoration and addition received the James B. Recchie Design Award from the Columbus Landmarks Foundation. The Columbus Metropolitan Library has grown to an institution with twenty branches in addition to the main library, and houses a collection of more than three million items. It was ranked number one in the United States in 2008 for the third time since 1999, based on circulation, user visits, attention to special populations, and digital access, among other criteria. The Peter Pan Fountain was added to the Grant Avenue entrance in 1928 by businessman Charles Munson, whose son George died at age six; the fountain was dedicated to all the children of Columbus.

The historic Great Southern Hotel, completed in 1896, is seen at the center right in this 1903 photo. Built by a consortium of German brewers and businessmen (including retail magnate Ralph Lazarus), it served as an announcement that the Germans had arrived in the business community. Nothing said more about the German business acumen than being able to build a fireproof hotel, especially after the destructive fire that consumed the Chittenden Hotel and two theaters just three years earlier. By 1915 the hotel had hosted William McKinley, Mark Hanna, William Taft, and Woodrow Wilson. With 225 rooms (of which 100 had private baths), a winter garden, a summer roof garden, an oyster restaurant, and an attached theater, it was one of the city's best hostelries. Over time, it became more of a residential hotel; humorist James Thurber's mother lived there. Four additional commercial buildings (with two outside the frame) date from between 1875 and 1900 and were built by members of the original partnership.

The Great Southern Hotel, now the Westin Columbus, is the only historic hotel in operation today in Columbus. The grand hotels—the Deshler, the Neil House, and the Pick-Fort Hayes Hotel—were demolished. Columbus has lost all of its other historic hotels but has a penchant for creating "new" historic hotels in old warehouse buildings. Having undergone major rehabilitation in 1985 and again a $10 million rehabilitation in the 1990s, the hotel exudes a splendor of the past with its spacious marble lobby and grand ballroom with original marble floor and stained-glass windows. The block of buildings adjacent to the hotel is listed in the National Register of Historic Places and is a cohesive sampling of the late-nineteenth-century Italianate style of commercial architecture with elaborate bracketed cornices, parapets, and storefronts constructed from a variety of materials—brick, cut stone, cast iron, and pressed metal. The buildings range from two to six stories, an amazing unbroken collection, and most were in place prior to the construction of the city's first skyscraper in 1897.

The Arsenal Building, popularly known as the Shot Tower, is one of two Civil War buildings still standing on this Civil War military base, historically known as the Columbus Arsenal (1860s), the Columbus Recruiting Depot (1901), and Fort Hayes (1922). The seventy-seven-acre site, all original forest along Harbor Road (now Cleveland Avenue), was owned by Robert Neil and was deeded to the government in 1861. The centerpiece of the property was the Shot Tower, which was designed to make ammunition, or shot, by dropping lead from the tower into vats of water below. However, by the time the tower was completed, technology had changed. The building was instead used for barracks and as a drill hall in inclement weather. Originally, ammunition was also stored in the tower's basement, to which the men sleeping above rightly objected. Most of the buildings on the base were added between the Spanish-American War and World War I, including the General's House, which still stands.

The Fort Hayes Historic District, listed in the National Register of Historic Places, consists of an unlikely combination of properties, including the Fort Hayes Metropolitan Education Center (a public magnet high school for students interested in the arts) and, until 2008, an active military base. The military site had been active since the Civil War. Fort Hayes is well known to local men who were inducted into the military during World War II and the Vietnam War. The officers' headquarters, club, and mess hall, along with two barracks buildings from the 1890s, have been artfully transformed into classrooms, science labs, small theaters, art rooms, and a student cafeteria. Both the Columbus City Schools and the long-range planning committee of the Fort Hayes Advisory Board received preservation awards at the state and local levels for nurturing the preservation of this historic campus.

By the late nineteenth century, Columbus had hundreds of passenger trains coming and going each day. A passing Shriners' parade or elephants from the Columbus-based Sells Brothers Circus (as seen in this 1898 photo) were a little rarer, but not unusual. As Henry Howe, an early Columbus historian, wrote, "The railroads, of course, run their tracks where they please . . . across the streets and thoroughfares . . . but as railroads go . . . when they run over a streetcar, a cab, or a citizen, they usually express regret." After two Union Stations were built at the ground level where railroad, pedestrian, and vehicular traffic met, and after a failed 1875 attempt at a tunnel under the tracks, the third Union Station was built on a viaduct over the tracks. Classically designed by Daniel Burnham, famous for the architecture of the 1893 World's Columbian Exposition in Chicago, the new Union Station's paired and fluted Corinthian columns, cherub statues, and arched facade were set over small shops on the east side of High Street. It was one of only two Burnham-designed buildings in Columbus.

Union Station was torn down in 1976. Its loss sparked the formation of the Columbus Landmarks Foundation. The contemporary Hyatt Regency Hotel and the Ohio Center (1980) were built on the site of Columbus's former Beaux Arts–style train station. North of the hotel, the Greater Columbus Convention Center was built in 1993 and expanded in 2000. Architect Peter Eisenman designed the building's Deconstructivist-style exterior to appear fragmented into multiple units of different pastel colors. These units relate to the scale of the commercial buildings across the street in the North Market Historic District, listed in the Columbus Register of Historic Properties and the National Register of Historic Places. The rear facade of the center mimics the twisting and elongated old train sheds, but in pastel colors, prompting the *Washington Post*'s description: "colliding Necco Wafers." Today, there are no passenger trains, interurbans, or streetcars to serve Columbus, but the return of modern alternatives is being hotly debated.

When this photo was taken in 1945, this business node was already a hundred years old. In 1842 pioneer David Beers's sons, Solomon and George Washington Beers, officially laid out a town along the Sandusky Pike (North High). Located about halfway between downtown Columbus and Worthington, it was the perfect transportation stop. During the Civil War, Camp Thomas was located near the intersections of present-day North High Street and Arcadia Avenue. For a while, General Lew Wallace, author of

*Ben-Hur*, commanded there. Several Civil War buildings still stand throughout the commercial and residential areas. North Columbus remained a distinct and separate community from Columbus until the late nineteenth century. When annexed, street names had to be changed—Columbus already had a First, Second, Third, and Fourth street, so Tompkins, Hudson, Duncan, and Dodridge streets were born. Located just south of "dry" Clintonville, North Columbus did a brisk business in the 1920s with no less than nine speakeasies.

North Columbus remains architecturally distinct from other commercial stretches on North High, with many Italianate and Victorian commercial buildings, some dating from the 1860s. The former Hudson and High Pharmacy is a popular neighborhood restaurant today. Families who helped to found North Columbus still live in the area or take interest in the future of the settlement. As a prosperous town, North Columbus had a dry-goods store, banks, furniture companies, a church, a nickelodeon theater, streetcar barns and turnarounds, fraternal lodges, and blacksmith shops. Today, the modern counterparts continue with small businesses that cater to neighborhood needs, plus a selection of specialty shops. Major infrastructure improvements are currently underway, and the Olde North Columbus Preservation Society is the caretaker.

Daniel Burnham was already a nationally known architect when he was wooed to Columbus to design the new Union Station in 1893, in the hopes of securing his services in the construction of what would become Columbus's first steel-framed skyscraper, the Wyandotte Building. Columbus was experiencing architectural envy after the firm of Burnham and Root designed the 1890 Society for Savings Building on Cleveland's Public Square. After the Chicago Fire of 1871, Burnham's signature buildings filled the city's skyline. His Chicago style was more eclectic, adding classicism and ornamentation. Following the 1893 World's Columbian Exposition, many cities desired a Burnham-designed building. The most arresting feature of the Wyandotte is the use of bay windows designed to gain maximum light for interior offices despite being located in urban canyons filled with tall buildings, but up close one can find understated but significant terra-cotta, stone, and brass ornamentation. The bay windows also make the facade of the building change with the light and the seasons. The State of Ohio purchased the building for much-needed office space in 1917.

The Wyandotte Building, listed in the National Register of Historic Places, was renovated in 1978. Appropriately, the building is home to the local chapter of the American Institute of Architects. Although dwarfed by the many skyscrapers and high-rise buildings constructed over the course of the past century, the Wyandotte Building remains a temple in its own right as the first skyscraper. It is the only remaining structure designed by Burnham in Columbus. The back side of the Huntington Bank Building can be seen in both images.

The complex of medical buildings across from Goodale Park was the ancestor to both Riverside Methodist Hospital (1961) on Olentangy River Road and a major college of medicine, the Ohio State University. In 1891 the Ohio Medical University was established and the first classes were held in a mansion at 775 Park Street. The mansion expanded that same year, and Protestant Hospital was built next door, along with more additions. In 1907

the Ohio Medical University and Starling Medical College merged into Starling-Ohio Medical College, and by 1914 it was known as the Ohio State University College of Medicine. The Protestant Hospital continued on; once supported by many church denominations, it was eventually supported by only the Methodists, and in 1922 became White Cross Hospital. On this site, it expanded from seventy-nine beds to more than 500.

When White Cross Hospital's buildings were razed in 1961 and the land was sold, proceeds went to support the work of Riverside Methodist Hospital (which has a white cross on its facade). The Victorian Gate is a newly constructed mixed-use project built on the site of White Cross Hospital. The development extends the full block between Park and North High streets to the east. The neighborhood called the Short North is centered on the commercial activity of North High Street and extends into the historic residential neighborhoods of Victorian Village and Italian Village. In 1984 Sandy Wood of the Wood Companies, a developer who had a vision for the area and stepped up to deliver it, began rehabilitating buildings. His objective was to do quality historic renovations to attract sophisticated tenants but keep rents low for emerging artists and gallery owners. The Short North is a revitalized historic urban neighborhood with restaurants, small boutiques and shops, art galleries, and private residences.

Clinton Elementary School was originally built to educate all the Clinton Township students who lived north of Mock Road (Hudson Avenue) and east of the North Columbus Pike (North High Street), as well as all the Clinton Township elementary students who lived north of Olentangy Street and west of the railroad tracks. The first building, constructed in 1895, cost $6,000; in 1904 the second building (at right), designed by architect David Riebel, who designed a number of Columbus schools, cost twice that amount. Columbus schools were bursting at the seams by 1913. More than a thousand new students entered the school system each year because of the unprecedented growth of the city. This was especially true of the city's north side and into Clintonville, and was also due to a new compulsory education law. By 1922 a third Clinton School building (seen here on the left) was added, and the 1895 building was eventually razed.

The Classical Revival 1904 school building, a former Clinton Township school, was brought into the Columbus City School District around 1912. It has had no additions and retains its historic character and details, including the symmetrical design, classically detailed and recessed central entry, and the pediment at the roofline. Today, Clinton Elementary is a public school with more than 300 students. The other 1922 school building on this parcel, oriented to North High Street, can be seen to the left and rear in this photo.

The most prominent building on Dennison Avenue, on the west side of Goodale Park, was the Sells mansion, seen here in 1897. The house's architectural style is affectionately known as "Circus Gothic" because its owner, Peter Sells, and his brothers Ephraim, Allen, and Lewis created one of the largest traveling circuses of the time. The success of the Sells Brothers Circus made them rivals to Barnum and Bailey and the Ringling Brothers, which eventually bought them out. They traveled with nearly fifty railroad cars for the big top and other tents, more than 400 employees, and fifty cages of animals. Winter quarters were in Columbus, on the west side of the Olentangy River in an area known as Sellsville (annexed to Columbus in the 1920s as Gypsyland). Peter Sells's mansion did not bring the happiness he had hoped for when it was built for his bride; their marriage ended in a scandalous divorce, and the house, which had cages in the basement for baby animals born in the winter months, eventually became a nursery school and day care.

The Dennison Avenue streetscape, fronting Goodale Park, is virtually unchanged. The neighborhood fell into disrepair in the 1960s and 1970s but has experienced a rebirth since then. The notable Peter Sells house at number 755 has had some physical changes with the removal of the gabled dormers. It has been restored as a single-family home. The area is located immediately north of downtown in the southern part of both the Near North Side Historic District, listed in the National Register of Historic Places, and the locally listed Victorian Village Historic District. As an area with local design review, commissioners and residents alike work hard to find a balance that permits compatible new construction, as well as sensitive rehabilitation within the district's boundaries, in the interest of encouraging reinvestment and protecting those characteristics that make the neighborhood distinctive.

Robert Neil built his mansion in 1856 on an Indian mound overlooking the Olentangy River valley, or what would become East Fifteenth and Indianola avenues. Neil's parents were William and Hannah Neil, whose homestead would become the Ohio State University. Robert's brother Henry inherited the house in 1870. Henry gave the City of Columbus, and especially the University District, a very prolific word—"Indianola." He was the first Ohioan to enlist in the Civil War for the Union, and was wounded at the

Battle of Iuka near Indianola, Mississippi. His house was then known as Indianola and the curved carriage path to his door became Iuka Avenue. The name Indianola is now attached to the city-registered historic district of Indianola Forest, two schools, a major street, and many churches and businesses. Iuka is a boulevard park that winds through the Iuka Historic District, listed in both the Columbus Register of Historic Properties and the National Register of Historic Places.

Today the former Neil mansion is home to the Alpha Sigma chapter of the Kappa Sigma fraternity, established in 1895 at the Ohio State University. The house was first leased by the fraternity in 1908 and then purchased in 1919. How the fraternity was able to lease the house is a story of charity with a touch of urban legend. According to the story, two Kappa Sigma brothers took it upon themselves to help an intoxicated man who had been robbed arrive home safely. In gratitude for their kind deed, the victim, a leasing agent

for the house, helped the fraternity to acquire the former mansion. The fraternity undertook a major remodeling of the house in 1938 and again in 1966. The 1930s effort resulted in the formal two-story Neoclassical Revival portico with large Doric columns and white dress coat. It is quite remarkable that the original Robert and Henry Neil house still stands within the confines of the fraternity, and that it has been served by its Kappa Sigma caretakers for more than a hundred years.

Indianola Swimming Pool, Indianola Park,
Columbus, Ohio.

Indianola Park, the brainchild of real-estate man Charles Miles, opened in 1904 with a swimming pool measuring 140 by 238 feet. Four artesian wells fed the pool, drawing in 30,000 gallons of water each hour through compressed air. Swimming instructors were employed each season, yet many women were too modest to enter the pool. A covered canopy from the bathhouse to the pool allowed women to enter the water discreetly. On hot days, the pool was cooled by chunks of floating ice. When the North Fourth streetcar line ended short of the park, Miles gathered equipment and a crew on a Saturday (when no court would be in session if he was arrested) and extended the line by Monday. Indianola Park also had the Blue Streak, one and half miles of roller coaster on four tiers. Water rides were a favorite, along with a working model of the Panama Canal. Vaudeville acts, a flea circus, and dance bands brought new crowds to the pavilion. The pavilion closed in 1937, when amusement parks at the end of streetcar lines were no longer popular.

Indianola Park met its demise along with the streetcar that gave birth to it. The park closed by the 1920s and the land was sold to the Columbus Board of Education for the development of Indianola Junior High School. Indianola's eleven-acre playground was once part of the park. The North Fourth Street swimming pool lasted until World War II, when it was filled in. The pool is now under the parking lot seen here. The bathhouse, now stripped of its towers and balconies, is best remembered as the home of an Albers Grocery.

The corner market was a drugstore and small luncheonette. When the Albers Grocery closed in the 1970s, the large structure had a number of uses, including a thrift store. The original owners of the property, members of a temperance society, would not allow establishments with liquor licenses. Within the last two years, the bathhouse has not only survived but is thriving as a center for a faith-based group that has even opened a coffeehouse for Ohio State students.

On July 8, 1929, Amelia Earhart and nineteen other dignitaries, including Henry and Edsel Ford and Harvey Firestone, arrived in Columbus from New York City by an Airway Limited train, disembarking on a specially constructed siding near this control tower. They left again to arrive in Los Angeles by trimotor planes and other trains, crossing the country in under forty-eight hours. With their arrival, Port Columbus's new airport was officially dedicated. That same day, Charles Lindbergh selected the airport as the vital eastern transfer point for the first transcontinental air-rail system. American Airlines, Trans World Airlines, and Lake Central Airlines sent out sixty-eight flights each day. In World War II, the U.S. government emphasized the strategic importance of Port Columbus by improving runways and taxiways for the building of a $4 million naval air station, used as an aircraft manufacturing plant. The success of the airport countered the initial skepticism of the citizens of Columbus, who had defeated a levy for its construction in 1927.

After the new terminal at Port Columbus opened in 1958, this original terminal building was abandoned. It is currently owned by the Columbus Regional Airport Authority and is leased for office space. The building is listed in the National Register of Historic Places, and recently a new state historic marker was dedicated at the site. A new twenty-one-story air-traffic control tower was dedicated in 2004, in time for Port Columbus International Airport's seventy-fifth anniversary.

Harry Daugherty was attorney general in the White House cabinets of presidents Warren G. Harding and Calvin Coolidge. Harding made many unwise choices by surrounding himself with scandalous friends, including Daugherty, who in the 1920s was acquitted of charges to defraud the United States government. From the 1890s, Daugherty lived in many places in Columbus until he built 481 East Town Street (seen here on the left) in 1904. He maintained a law practice in the prestigious Wyandotte Building downtown until his death in 1941. Daugherty's neighbor at home was also his neighbor at work. Frank Davis, a utilities lawyer and capitalist, lived in the Chateauesque-style home at 475 East Town (on the right); Daugherty and Davis had suites next to each other in the Wyandotte. The interior of Davis's mansion is opulent, but not many know that the gem is a second-story sunporch that is—top to bottom, fixtures to floors, walls to fireplace—done in Arts and Crafts–style Rookwood tile.

Both houses are located in the East Town Street Historic District, across from the Topiary Park and the site of the old Ohio School for the Deaf. The district is listed in both the Columbus Register of Historic Properties and the National Register of Historic Places. Both former residential properties are zoned for use as offices. The highly regarded Columbus College of Art and Design (CCAD) unexpectedly inherited the Davis mansion in June 2007 from Ronald Sloter, the president of a concrete company. As sole beneficiary of his estate, CCAD is poised to inherit the $1 million mansion that Sloter had just acquired in 1997, in addition to the antiques and art within the house, valued at $4.1 million. However, the school is not yet counting its blessings, as the gift is being held up in litigation; Sloter's sister has sued the estate.

State institutions made Columbus famous and added to Ohio's reputation for progressive treatment. The High Victorian Gothic Ohio School for the Deaf opened in 1868 and an additional gymnasium building (left) was built in 1888–98 in a distinctive French Normandy style. State institutions with impressive architecture and well-tended gardens were considered amenities in the upscale residential Town-Franklin neighborhood that developed after the Civil War. The Ohio School for the Deaf joined with the Ohio School for the Blind in the move to new facilities on North High Street in the 1950s. The loss of the larger building in 1981 preceded the loss of another—and the most impressive—of the state institutions. The State Asylum for the Insane, the largest institution of its kind in the world when it was constructed (and the largest brick building in the United States until the Pentagon was built), was razed in the 1990s. The asylum cost $1.3 million at the time of its construction in 1870.

In the 1950s, the two school buildings housed state offices. The larger one, badly neglected for decades, burned in a mysterious fire in 1981, just as it was being considered for senior citizen housing. The city acquired the remaining property, which was leased to a developer who renovated it for offices. The most interesting development of the park is the award-winning Topiary Garden, designed in 1992 by James and Elaine Mason, who worked for the Columbus Department of Recreation and Parks. Based on French painter Georges Seurat's *A Sunday on La Grande Jatte*, the park continues to receive national attention. Campus Apartments of Philadelphia is currently proposing to adapt the remaining school building for student housing. Contributing to the urban park setting is the ornate nineteenth-century cast-iron fence surrounding the acreage that had originally been installed at the statehouse. The building is listed in the Columbus Register of Historic Properties and the National Register of Historic Places.

Eddie Rickenbacker was born here on October 8, 1890, one of seven children. He went to work at age twelve when his father died, developed a passion for mechanics, and took a correspondence course in engineering and drafting. By age twenty, he was a top race car driver, winning championships at national and international meets. In 1917 he enlisted in the U.S. Army, and his first job was driving General John J. Pershing's car, but within months he began preliminary training for flying. In the 94th Pursuit Squadron of the U.S. Air Service in World War I, Rickenbacker scored twenty-seven kills, making him the leading air ace of the American forces that fought against the "German Flying Circus" and the Red Baron, Manfred von Richthofen. After the war, he was associated with the Rickenbacker car and later Cadillac, but he left to make his mark with North American Aviation Inc. In the 1930s Rickenbacker became president of Eastern Airlines. He always listed the correspondence course on engineering and drafting as his only educational experience.

The exterior of Eddie Rickenbacker's boyhood home was recently rehabilitated as the first step in a long-term plan to create the Rickenbacker-Woods Technology Center to promote science, innovation, and technology. The house has been threatened time and again by neglect, deterioration, demolition, and proposed relocation. As early as 1958 there was talk by city leaders about establishing a museum here. In 1998, forty years later, the City of Columbus purchased the building and identified funds to stabilize it and acquire adjacent property for the technology center, named for two of Columbus's famous sons, Rickenbacker and Granville T. Woods, a prolific inventor. In addition to being one of only three National Historical Landmarks in the city, the house is also listed in the National Register of Historic Places and the Columbus Register of Historic Properties.

The history of the First Baptist Church in Columbus stretches to the roots of the early city. Founded in 1831 by eleven men (including three African Americans), the Baptists were the fifth denomination to establish themselves in Columbus, after the Presbyterians, the Methodists, the Episcopalians, and the Lutherans. The Baptists had outgrown four other facilities (starting with their log church on Mound Street between South High and Front streets), and in only six decades had grown sufficiently to purchase a lot for $14,000 and build a church for $50,000 in 1896. At its height in the 1920s, about 1,200 people worshipped here each Sunday and thousands more listened to the service as it was broadcast over WMAN, the church's early radio station. The mother church helped to give birth to no less than a dozen other Baptist churches, including the Second Baptist Church in 1836, an African American Baptist congregation.

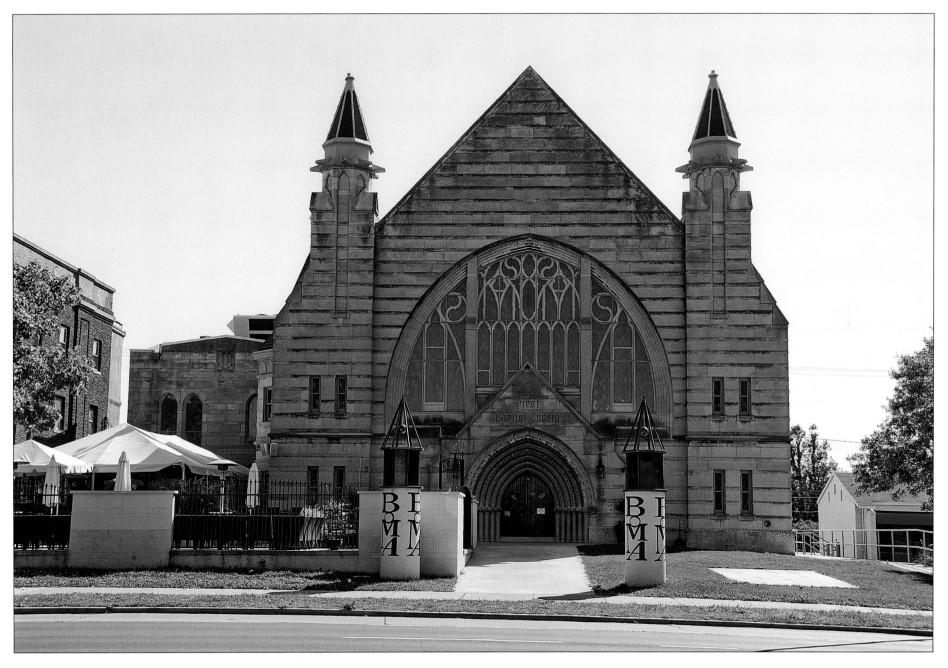

Success is sometimes not rewarding; by its 175th anniversary in 1999, the First Baptist Church had just 100 members. The First Baptist Church was creatively reborn after it was sold and repurposed as the Bar of Modern Art, following a $5 million renovation in 2006. Otherwise known as "BoMA," a high-end nightclub, art gallery, and restaurant, it has recently transitioned once again into an exclusive special-events venue. Multiple levels, dance floors, artist-designed bars, original stained-glass windows, and an outdoor patio add to the unique ambience.

State institutions of great size and grandeur sprang up almost simultaneously after the Civil War as Ohio established itself as possibly the most progressive state in the union in the care and treatment of citizens with special needs. In 1836 it was determined that there were 202 blind persons in Ohio. Dr. Samuel Howe, director of the New England Institution for the Blind in Boston, arrived with several pupils at the request of the Ohio legislature. They demonstrated how the blind could be taught in letters and mechanical arts—and the first school opened in 1837 with one teacher and five students. Their efforts grew into the establishment of the State Asylum for the Blind, authorized by the Ohio legislature in 1869. The new building followed the institutional architecture of the day when it was built at Main Street and Parsons Avenue in 1874. Humorist James Thurber, whose grandfather lived across the street, remembered playing baseball on the grounds. It is shown here in 1889.

Although missing its multiple towers, the old Ohio State School for the Blind continues to have a commanding presence in its parklike setting. The Ohio State School for the Blind, like its counterpart for deaf students, moved out of the downtown area in the 1950s. Various state offices inhabited this 240,000-square-foot institutional complex of buildings; one major tenant was the Ohio Department of Public Safety. After years of vacancy, the complex was rehabilitated in 2002 to consolidate the City of Columbus Department of Health offices. A former chapel was converted to an elegant community meeting space with vaulted ceilings. The small touches original to the buildings, such as the raised bumps on the stairway handrails to enable children to count their way down the steps, were discovered. Several wings to the east were taken down for a new parking deck, and a modern but complementary entryway was created on the eastern addition. The school building is now listed in the National Register of Historic Places.

By the early nineteenth century, Columbus was no longer a village in which neighbors might take in an orphaned or abandoned child. Hannah Neil—wife of William Neil, one of the richest men in Columbus—and three others organized the Industrial School Association in 1858. By 1862 some of the group formed a school of twenty-four boys, and in four years the school grew to 400 children. The group organized "Mothers' Meetings" for women to learn housekeeping and sewing, a Female Benevolent Society (which still exists), and with $12,000 they bought the Neville home on East Friend Street (now Main Street) in 1868. They received foundlings, also known as "basket babies," who were left at the door. One man arrived with five small children, a newborn (whose mother had died in childbirth), and a cow. Hannah Neil died in 1878, and the school with the grim name was renamed the Hannah Neil Mission and the Home for the Friendless to honor its founder.

Virtually unchanged from the 1933 image, including the intact iron fence that surrounds the property, the Hannah Neil Home for Children now serves as the offices for the Ohio Arts Council, and has for many years. The Ohio Arts Council is a state agency that provides financial assistance to artists and arts organizations and supports quality arts programs with the goal of strengthening Ohio communities culturally, educationally, and economically.

Franklin Park was once the site of the county fairgrounds, purchased for that purpose in 1851 by the Franklin County Agricultural Society. For thirty years, it remained the place for showcasing Franklin County's agricultural products. In 1886, by an act of the state legislature, it became a public park, to be administered jointly by the county and the city. In 1895 a conservatory was erected in the park (see inset), which cost $24,000 and was designed by Columbus architect John Freese. The T-shaped building underwent a major alteration in the 1950s when an original Beaux Arts–style arched opening with classical pilasters was removed. A more functional vestibule was added. From its opening through the 1970s especially, the park was the place for agricultural displays, romantic walks, and political rallies and addresses— from General William T. Sherman's famous "War is hell" speech to civil rights demonstrations and community celebrations.

The Franklin Park Conservatory, a premier horticultural institution, showcases exotic plant collections and special exhibitions, and offers educational programs. The elegant iron-and-glass Palm House of the conservatory, listed in the National Register of Historic Places, was expanded and renovated between 1989 and 1992, and the park served as the official site for the 500th anniversary of Christopher Columbus's voyage to the Americas. A permanent work, *Light Raiment II*, by renowned light artist James Turrell, was installed in 2008, dramatically bathing the exterior of the Palm House in colored lighting in the evening. The conservatory displays its collection of work by glass artist Dale Chihuly, creatively interspersed throughout the complex. The thirty-foot stainless-steel sculpture seen in the foreground, entitled *NavStar* by Stephen Canneto, represents a ship's sails, one of which points to the North Star, and was unveiled for the 1992 AmeriFlora horticulture exposition.

In 1849 the City of Columbus constructed the Market House on a large lot between Town and Rich streets. Since there was no city hall, city offices occupied the second floor. Along both sides of the market were 388 feet of brick and limestone walls fronted by produce and meat stalls. Merchants on the first floor sold pigeons, chickens, quail, squirrels, rabbits, cherries, blackberries, apples, and other locally produced goods starting as early as six in the morning. On Saturday night at nine o'clock, a bell was rung and merchants could sell their remaining items at any price. In the 1880s, many of the farmers and butchers stayed at the Farmers Hotel (circa 1870) across the street, where rooms were only 35 cents a night. Robert F. Wolfe of the Wolfe Brothers Shoe Company, *Ohio State Journal*, and later the *Columbus Dispatch*, stayed here when he first came to Columbus. In the center of this 1897 view, the Norwich Hotel's distinctive tower is seen. The Norwich might not have been built as a hotel, but by 1899, it appears in city directories as a hotel of the highest quality.

As many as 20,000 people might shop at the Central Market on a Saturday in the 1940s; however, this was not enough to keep the market from destruction as part of the Market-Mohawk urban renewal in the 1960s. The twenty-four-story Chase Bank seen in the distance was built in 1964–65 as the Columbus Center. Designed by Harrison and Abramovitz of New York City, it was the second modern high-rise office building introduced to the city's skyline. There was a lull of almost forty years in skyscraper construction between when the LeVeque Tower (American Insurance Union Citadel) was built in 1924 and when this new generation of skyscrapers began in 1963 with the twenty-story glass-and-steel Key Bank Building. The Norwich Hotel managed to survive and has been renovated into offices. Many of the commercial fronts on South Fourth and State streets were altered in the 1930s, obscuring terra-cotta cornices and cast-iron columns.

The large store sign in this circa-1900 photo of South High Street is the clue that Lazarus will soon be making another bold move. A new type of department store was about to replace many small shops downtown. The original Lazarus, located several storefronts to the right, was a modest, one-room shop where Simon Lazarus had established himself as a men's and boys' clothier, and also as an acting rabbi and founding member of Temple Israel. With the end of the Civil War, clothing manufacturers had no business in uniforms. With good merchandising and clever tactics, Lazarus was able to acquire properties to the south and added boots and shoes, and eventually women's clothes. The storefronts were made to look like one building, with electric lights on the facade at night, and a clock tower with a whistle for signaling weather conditions. When Lazarus died in 1877, his sons, Fred and Ralph, succeeded him and planned a new store on the northwest corner of West Town and South High streets. The new Lazarus store opened in 1909.

The one-story, nineteenth-century commercial buildings stood on South High Street into the early twentieth century. At the intersection of South High and Walnut Street (now closed), a three-story commercial block, the Hi-Walnut Building, was built in 1924, replacing the two one-story buildings on the site. The building to its north appears to be the southern end of a row of three- and four-story buildings that had a prominent, illuminated clock tower on top—the first Lazarus Department Store, which was on the site from 1895 until 1909.

This piece of the assemblage of buildings that masqueraded as one store remained in the Lazarus family until 1967. To the north, the Ohio National Bank sits on the southwest corner of East Town and South High streets, where it once occupied part of the 1895 Lazarus Building. After Lazarus moved into its new store, the bank built the Neoclassical Revival building in 1930. Although the Lazarus store closed in 2004, the 1909 Lazarus Building (far right) has been rehabilitated for offices and certified for its environmentally friendly approach.

The town of Franklinton dates to 1797 and helped give birth to the city of Columbus in 1812. By 1908 Franklinton was annexed to Columbus and remained a distinct neighborhood. Nicknamed "the Bottoms" in reference to its proximity to the confluence of two rivers, the Scioto and Olentangy, Franklinton's worst enemy was the constant threat of flooding. This 1908 photo was used to illustrate how bad things had become. A grand mall, running from east to west, was planned. Neoclassical in design and heavily influenced by the City Beautiful movement, it was to be a renovation of the old neighborhood and a more sightly approach to the capitol (seen in the distance). The 1913 flood, however, incited the urban renewal. The mall did not materialize, though the riverfront and the vision of a neoclassical downtown remained. Franklinton, now minus the factories (and slums) on the river, settled in to be a modest area. A federally funded flood wall was built in the 1990s but has never been tested on the 100-year floodplain.

The capitol can no longer be seen from this location, looking east from West State Street. Most immediately obstructing the view is the Center of Science and Industry (COSI), which moved into the historic Central High School (built as the first piece of the new civic center in the 1920s). COSI's relocation in 1999 necessitated the loss of the school's auditorium and threatened a 1940s WPA mural by Emerson Burkhart painted above the proscenium. The mural, titled *Music*, had largely been forgotten because the principal had deemed it to be too "racy" and had it whitewashed. Ten thirteen-foot panels were removed, and students from the Fort Hayes Metropolitan Education Center and teacher Teresa Weidenbusch led the five-year project to restore the mural, the largest WPA mural to be restored in the country. *Music* now hangs in the Ohio Center. Also visible in the skyline is the Ohio Judicial Center, the Vern Riffe Center for Government and the Arts (1989), the Fifth Third Center (1998), and the Huntington Center (1998).

Inspired by West Side civic associations, the Alumni Association of West High School, and Judge C. J. Randall, the Columbus Board of Education decided to build a new high school on Powell Avenue. Prior to 1908, West Side students attended Central High, but in 1908 the first West High (now Starling Middle School) was built on Starling Street. Construction on this second high school, located farther to the west, began in 1926 and the school opened in 1929. Architect Howard Dwight Smith had already won fame for his design of Ohio Stadium at the Ohio State University.

The Georgian Revival West High School was one of five high schools (and eleven other buildings) built as part of a new $10 million building campaign for the Columbus Public Schools in the 1920s. West High retains its historic character and details. Four of the high schools built in this decade (West, East, North, and South) are among the top-rated historic school buildings evaluated by the Columbus Landmarks Foundation for the school system. In 2002 all schools in use in the district that were at least forty years old were inventoried and assessed. The criteria for evaluation of the fifty-six schools included age, significance, and architectural integrity; this comprehensive understanding of the historic importance of school buildings helps guide difficult decisions for school leadership. West High School alumni maintain a hall of fame that honors distinguished graduates and includes nationally known figures such as singer Nancy Wilson (1954) and astronaut Donn Eisele (1948).

Many of Columbus's nineteenth-century elementary public school buildings sported magnificent towers, considered de rigueur as educational symbols and necessary for good ventilation, though by the late nineteenth century, taxpayers increasingly saw them as architectural follies and highly wasteful. One of the most striking is the 1891 Avondale School, built at a cost of nearly $49,000; the site cost $3,600. Its sixteen rooms housed 421 students and thirteen teachers and drew some of the city's neediest children from the Scioto River to Martin Avenue. During the March 1913 flood that devastated many parts of Ohio, seven school buildings, including Avondale, were put out of use and five of the twenty-three children who died were students at Avondale. Columbus has often been noted for its educational firsts—including having the first kindergarten in the United States in 1838, creating the first junior high (Indianola) in 1909, and being one of the first cities to employ a school superintendent.

This monumental block-type school designed by Columbus City Schools' architect, David Riebel, in the Richardsonian Romanesque style has experienced little change in more than a century, serving as an elementary school for West Side students. The only major change in the building has been the removal of two ornate towers from the peak of the roof. In the 1880s and 1890s, new attendance laws made education compulsory for children from eight to fourteen years of age. These laws led to a sizable increase in enrollment and account for

a large number of Riebel-designed schools in this period. Avondale School is one of several historic public school buildings that Columbus City Schools has recently rehabilitated and expanded, responding to recommendations regarding the historic significance of schools made by the Columbus Landmarks Foundation. Avondale was one of the sixteen top-ranked significant historic elementary school buildings in the district. Ten of the sixteen were elementary school buildings constructed in the nineteenth century.

The destruction of the houses on Cypress Avenue, some distance from the confluence of the Olentangy and Scioto rivers, marks the magnitude of the 1913 flood. The West Side had experienced a number of floods in its history; the village continued to push back farther from the river and reestablish itself each time. The 1898 flood was so devastating to the West Side that no one suspected it would be only fifteen years later that the largest flood recorded on Ohio's 100-year floodplain would hit. A week of heavy rains, combined with frozen March ground, caused the earthen banks that protected Franklinton to easily give way. Within hours, water rose into second floors of houses. All vehicular bridges collapsed. Men who worked on the east side of the river left their stranded families. At least ninety-four people died and some bodies were never recovered. At the extreme left in this 1913 photo is Engine House No. 10, built in 1897, which continued to operate through the crisis.

To this day, no structures have replaced the two houses in this Franklinton neighborhood that were uprooted by the devastating 1913 flood. The house at the far right, however, remains intact, although it no longer struts a front porch or a third-story corner tower. Engine House No. 10 can still be seen at the far left in this photo. This new station was built in 2007 to complement the original station, which had been built in 1896–97. In 2008 city officials dedicated the Maurice Gates Memorial and Engine House No. 10, the city's

oldest operating fire station in historic Franklinton, as the city's first "green" fire station to meet environmentally friendly LEED (Leadership in Energy and Environmental Design) standards. The Maurice Gates Memorial honors a young firefighter from the Franklinton area and Engine House No. 10 who died in the line of duty on September 15, 1984, during a warehouse fire. The memorial was funded by the Franklinton community and members of Maurice Gates's recruit class.

From this modest building on West Broad Street next to the Colonial Theater, the American Insurance Union (AIU) lobbied the state legislature against child labor and for safety in the workplace. The common man was important to this fraternal beneficiary association, which issued policies for life, health, and accident insurance because working-class families were its bread and butter. By 1915 it was extremely well positioned financially. In an era of progressive reform, AIU president John Lentz stood out as a moral man who would not invest with anyone engaged in liquor traffic or lend any funds for the distribution of alcohol. Lentz could sell just about anything to anyone, and he sold Columbus on the idea of a skyscraper. For years, Columbus citizens did not see much progress behind the high fence that surrounded the site of the former AIU Building. Sandhogs—workers from New York's tunnels—were brought in to work so far below the surface that a special hospital was built on-site to minimize their decompression sickness.

The AIU Citadel, at 555 feet 6 inches tall, was clearly the tallest building in Ohio when it was built. The AIU Citadel took two men's dreams, 600 workers, three years, and five lives to build. Completed in 1927, the striking building was the tangible result of efforts from John Lentz and architect C. Howard Crane of Detroit, who translated civic duty into Columbus's most recognizable skyscraper. The AIU was hit hard by the Great Depression and went into receivership seven years after the building's opening. By 1946 the building was called the Lincoln-LeVeque Tower, named for owners John Lincoln, president of Cleveland's Lincoln Electric, and multimillionaire real estate developer Frederick LeVeque. In 1977, after the tragic death of her husband, Katherine LeVeque championed the caretaker role of the tower and the adjacent Palace Theatre until selling the property in 2005. The LeVeque Tower is listed in the Columbus Register of Historic Properties and the National Register of Historic Places.

St. Patrick's Church, founded in 1852, is the second-oldest Catholic church in Columbus, established at Naghten and Seventh (Grant) streets. Located in the heart of what came to be known as "Irish Broadway," the parish provided acculturation for newly arrived Irish, many of whom sought work with the building of the Ohio and Erie Canal and the National Road after fleeing the Great Famine in Ireland. American nativism flared with Irish immigration and sparked rioting, arson, and even murder in the East and in parts of Ohio.

Central Ohio was not spared—a Chillicothe convent was attacked by a mob, postmasters destroyed bundles of the *Catholic Telegraph*, and Columbus's bishop, Sylvester H. Rosecrans, bravely quelled a riot in Cincinnati. But in Columbus, it was Irish and Germans who sought their separate spheres in life and death—the church cemetery had separate Irish and German sections. St. Patrick's was embraced by the Irish as their own and three St. Patrick's priests went on to become bishops. A school building (see inset) was added in 1854.

The St. Patrick's school reached peak enrollment in 1891 and closed in 1959. The church was nearly destroyed by a raging fire in 1935. Within a year, the church was reconstructed and included new pews carved with shamrocks, reflecting the Irish heritage of the original congregation. In 2003 the church was renovated, the school was demolished, and a new parish center was built to be compatible with the historic church and rectory. In 1866 overcrowding at St. Patrick's and the desire for a more centrally located church led to St.

Patrick's Reverend Edward Fitzgerald to lay the groundwork for building a new church. Two years later, the Roman Catholic Diocese of Columbus was established by the Vatican. Reverend Fitzgerald's initiative to build a new church resulted in the construction of what would become St. Joseph's Cathedral on East Broad and Fifth streets, home of the Diocese of Columbus, consecrated in 1878.

The corner of North Fourth Street (right) and Warren Street (left) was the gateway to a working-class and immigrant community, annexed into Columbus during the Civil War. Attached row houses and single-family brick houses with modest hood molds and lintels—popular trims at the time—predominated. Italians began to arrive in the late nineteenth century, some as skilled laborers to do masonry work or cut stone to build the new state buildings, the university, churches, and downtown businesses. Access to the Marble Cliff quarries was by the Fifth Avenue streetcar. The Jeffrey Manufacturing and Mining Company, founded in 1883, was the largest employer. Its complex was surrounded by a massive brick wall along North Fourth. The population was ethnically mixed: Greeks, Lebanese, and Polish joined the Italians. If they could afford it, families moved from Flytown on the west. The Irish, having arrived earlier than the Italians, were within walking distance of St. Patrick's, and the Italians' religious and community life centered on St. John the Baptist Church.

Following its closure, thirty-two of the Jeffrey Manufacturing Company's buildings were demolished in 1987. The distinctive long brick wall, running the length of the Jeffrey site, was lost. However, today this massive parcel is again the gateway for a thriving historic area and a new urban neighborhood built from the ground up—Jeffrey Place. Visible in the distance on the right are the Courtyard Townhomes, and behind are the Lofts at Jeffrey Place. The row houses on Warren Street, to the left, have been converted to condominiums. Nearby, large-scale commercial bakeries still operate, but the industries, like Jeffrey and the small businesses that supplied it, are gone. The Italian Village Society mobilized in 1972 against the deteriorating physical condition of the area and the threat of losing more historic buildings by demolition. In 1973 the Italian Village Commission was established by the Columbus City Council as part of a network of neighborhood commissions that serve as city advisory boards.

Neighborhood firehouses and organized teams of city employees trained in firefighting did not make much of an appearance in Columbus until just before the start of the Civil War. From about 1860 through the 1890s, impressive masonry fire stations like Engine House No. 5 (shown here in 1894) were built throughout the city. They usually included distinctive towers for drying fire hoses, second- and even third-floor living space for the firemen, massive doors for horse-drawn steam pumpers, and Gothic or Romanesque features. Before 1860, volunteer firefighters with bucket brigade lines or hand-operated pumps were used, drawing water from nearby cisterns, but when the original prestigious Neil House, across from the statehouse, burned to the ground in 1860, people got serious about fire protection. The Neil House had been adjacent to two cisterns and even had its own fire company. Volunteer firefighters and citizens were lucky to save the rest of the block.

Privately owned since 1970, the former Engine House No. 5 appears unchanged with the exception of the missing pyramidal roof atop the tower and gabled dormers with finials. It is one of several nineteenth-century firehouses standing throughout the city but no longer in use for their original purpose. Engine House No. 5 kept its historic name and was a premier seafood restaurant in the 1970s. Waiters used the fireman's pole for a dramatic entrance into the dining room to deliver birthday cakes to patrons. The building is used today as the offices of a marketing, research, and design firm.

On the corner of Thurman and City Park avenues, Dietrich Gruen began manufacturing watches in 1882 to provide stock for the watch shop he had opened in 1874. His high-quality watches included Swiss movements. By the early 1900s, Columbus Watch had relocated to Indiana. Henry Hallwood—mine engineer, inventor, paving-block manufacturer—used the two-story building for his Hallwood Cash Register Company. Hallwood's company and the National Cash Register Company in Dayton repeatedly sued each other between 1897 and 1912 for infringement and restraint of trade agreements. John Patterson, National Cash Register's president, was found guilty, fined, and sentenced to jail just as the 1913 flood hit Dayton. Patterson worked tirelessly in relief efforts and was seen as a hero. The court backed away from the sentence and eventually settlements were made. The H. C. Godman Shoe Company built the three-story building in 1920 and operated there until 1943.

The property was known as the Integrity Supply Company Office and Warehouse Complex, named for a manufacturer and wholesaler of plumbing fixtures that operated here from 1957 until 1997. The pair of early factory buildings and the neighborhood of German Village are listed in the Columbus Register of Historical Properties and the National Register of Historic Places.

They were recently packaged as a loft office complex called City Park Place and have approximately 50,000 square feet of space. The two-story brick building (see inset) currently houses legal offices and the three-story former factory houses multiple tenants.

In 1911 local doctors, including noted eye, ear, nose, and throat surgeon Dr. William Sloss Van Fossen, founded the St. Clair Hospital and School for Nursing. Designed to be a private general hospital, it opened with twenty-five beds and increased to fifty beds by 1918. After that year, the numbers dropped until there were only twenty-seven beds in 1930. However, with the Depression, the hospital saw some increases. In 1940 St. Clair Hospital was last listed as a "registered hospital," as defined by the American Medical Association, meaning that it was approved for internship training; in that same year, it became a convalescent home. Eight years later, it was turned into a hotel. A house next door once served as the residence and training school for nurses. In this era, there were a number of privately established hospitals, and only one—Grant Hospital—has survived to the present day.

St. Clair Hospital transitioned to a convalescent home in 1940 and to an African American–owned hotel in 1948. The Hotel St. Clair was one of the few accommodations where African Americans were permitted to stay by de facto segregation. A social center for the community, the hotel closed in 1976. In 2001 the building, which had fallen into disrepair, was resuscitated, listed in the National Register of Historic Places, took advantage of federal tax credits for the rehabilitation of historic buildings, and became senior citizen housing. An Ohio Historical Marker, researched by students from neighboring Monroe Middle School, was dedicated on the site in 2007, for which the students were given a Preservation Award by the Columbus Landmarks Foundation.

Benjamin Huntington, a prominent Columbus banker and businessman, descended from an ancestor who helped to start the American Revolution and another, Samuel, who was president of the Continental Congress. His brother Pelatiah sailed to Russia on a whaling ship at age fourteen, came to Columbus at seventeen as a messenger boy, and stayed to found the Huntington Bank in 1866. The French Second Empire–style mansion was owned by the Huntington family until 1927. It was built in the 1870s on land platted as East Park Place, seventy-two acres of which had previously been the site for the state's first mental asylum. The asylum, specified by the legislature to be at least one mile from the Ohio Statehouse, was built in 1836 but burned in 1868. Next door to the Huntington home was the mansion of Andrew Denny Rodgers, son-in-law of William Sullivant and president of the Columbus Consolidated Street Railway Company.

In 1927 these former prominent residences served as the first offices for the Ohio Farm Bureau Federation. The large addition to the back of the building dates from 1929. The Ohio Farm Bureau was the progenitor of Nationwide Insurance. The mansions sat vacant and deteriorated at the intersection of Interstate 71 and East Broad Street for years. The two houses were listed in the National Register of Historic Places and rehabilitated for offices in the late 1980s, and they continue to serve as offices today. The buildings sit at the southern gateway to the Jefferson Center for Learning and the Arts, an incubator for nonprofit organizations nurturing human services, education, and the arts, located along the Jefferson Avenue Historic District, which is also listed in the National Register of Historic Places. The Columbus Landmarks Foundation, the Columbus Historical Society, and the Thurber House are among the twenty-seven tenants in the district.

The Second Renaissance Revival–style Columbus Gallery of Fine Arts was designed by the Columbus architectural firm of Richards, McCarty, and Bulford in 1932, based on the drawings of Charles Platt, designer of the National Gallery in Washington, D.C. The roots of an art museum stretch back to the 1840 Francis Sessions mansion on East Broad Street, which stood at the site of the present museum. Sessions made his money in dry goods and banking, amassing enough to be a philanthropist for the homeless, libraries, abused animals, medical colleges, and the arts. He donated his home to form an art gallery and school, and upon his death in 1892, a substantial donation continued the work of the Columbus Art School (established in 1879) and early arts efforts. In 1923 the Gallery of Fine Arts merged with the Columbus Art Association to form the Columbus Gallery of Fine Arts. Sessions's neighbor, the advertising genius Frederick Schumacher, donated his substantial collection of works by the old masters to the museum.

When the existing building opened in 1932, it received extensive coverage in the architectural publications of the time, including high praise for the huge sculptural frieze, forty-eight feet long and almost five feet tall, depicting sixty-eight artists; it was designed by New Yorker Robert Aitken. A 1974 addition, designed by Van Buren and Firestone, was made possible through fund-raising efforts and the generosity of the Richard M. Ross family. The spacious grounds of the museum became the Museum Sculpture Park and the enclosed Sculpture Garden, both laid out by English landscape designer Russell Page in 1979. Now the Columbus Museum of Art, the building is on the National Register of Historic Places and is currently undergoing an $80 million capital and endowment campaign in the interest of expansion. The first phase began in 2009 with the rehabilitation of Beaton Hall into staff offices. Located to the rear of the museum, Beaton Hall's 1840s porch facade is a fragment of the Francis Sessions mansion previously on the site.

Tucked behind the former bathhouse of Indianola Park, the first junior high to have its own building was built from the designs of architect Howard Dwight Smith. The junior high movement started in Columbus in 1908, an educational collaborative experiment between the superintendent of Columbus City Schools, Jacob A. Shawan, and the president of the Ohio State University, William Oxley Thompson. They redesigned the first year of the high school curriculum, ninth grade, to be a capstone to the seventh and eighth grades, and housed the grades together. The plan was to combat the alarming dropout rate after eighth grade. The experiment worked, perhaps too well, and the original Indianola Junior High (still standing a few blocks away) became rapidly overcrowded. Indianola Junior High on Nineteenth Avenue was made possible by purchase of the land formerly used for Indianola Park, which had closed. Fortunately, the school, with many rich details, was built before the stock market crash and the Great Depression, and opened in 1929.

The junior high was replaced with a new educational concept, the middle school, which housed grades six through eight and returned ninth grade to the high schools. Indianola's interior and exterior details remain unusual in their richness, giving credit to its students' interest in their environment. Dr. Edwin Frey, a professor of fine arts at Ohio State, under the watchful eye of students who knew the carvings they helped select would be on their school in the fall, chose Chief Tahgajute (James Logan) of the Mingo tribe for the entablature.

Animals surround the door and terra-cotta tiles of flora and fauna adorn the exterior. Inside, the library's decorated plaster ceiling, stone carvings around the fireplace, and rich wood bookcases remain. The cafeteria has decorative plaster and leaded-glass bookcases. The school is listed in the Columbus Register of Historic Properties and the National Register of Historic Places, and was one of the top-ranked buildings for architectural and historical significance by Columbus City Schools and the Columbus Landmarks Foundation.

David Beers Sr., born in 1749, built the log cabin at North High Street and Dodridge Avenue after moving to Ohio from New Jersey in the 1790s. As a child, he and his younger sister had been captured by Native Americans, and David was taken into Canada. The family was separated; Beers was released at age fourteen at the end of the French and Indian War and settled in Pennsylvania. Later, he and his wife Elizabeth and nine children (with more to come) set out again for Ohio, eventually making their way to Clinton Township in Franklin County, where he built the county's first grist mill on the Olentangy River and a cabin up the hill on the Sandusky Pike (North High Street). Beers's ability to speak Native American languages helped establish the mill as a trading post. Beers witnessed the establishment of the United States and lived to the ripe old age of 104.

Beers's mill survived into the early twentieth century, and was a favorite for children to explore near the Olentangy Amusement Park on the river. Following a successful career as a competitive bicyclist and circus daredevil, Conn Baker settled down after meeting Laura Calvert, a popular English musical comedienne, while they were on tour in India. Baker and his brother, both artists, purchased the vacant Beers cabin and moved it to Norwich Avenue. Here he and his brother did landscape painting and created an

artist's studio on the second floor and filled the house with mementos from world travels. Poonah, the Bakers' daughter, named for the city in India where her parents were engaged, lived here with her sons, Conn and Kay, who inherited the cabin. Today the cabin is still owned and inhabited by members of the Baker family. The log cabin, although not on its original site, is the oldest building still standing in Franklin County.

The Henry C. Werner home on East Broad Street was built from 1908 to 1914. Werner was a boot and shoe manufacturer who owned, with partners, the Henry C. Werner Company and the Ferguson Rubber Heel Company (wholesale boots and shoes) on East Spring Street. Although Werner was not the largest of the manufacturers, his move from East Long Street to a house with a more prominent address testifies to Columbus's successful industry. A larger shoe manufacturer, H. C. Godman, also had his mansion on Broad Street. Shoe manufacturing was a big business in Columbus, aided by readily available leather and a central location on the railroad network for distribution. It was estimated that one out of every eight pairs of shoes worn in the United States in the early twentieth century was manufactured in Columbus.

This grand house overlooking Franklin Park has had only three owners: the Werners, who kept it until 1941; Frank and Linda Barrow; and Mary Brooks, who has owned it since 1973. The Werner-Brooks house is located on Columbus's quintessential grand street, East Broad, and is one of sixty structures that make up the East Broad Street Historic District, listed in the National Register of Historic Places since 1987. Buildings in the district range in date from the mid-nineteenth century to the mid-twentieth century and represent more than seventeen different styles of architecture.

In 1920 a private eighteen-bed hospital, primarily for African American patients, opened at 893 East Long Street. It was the first of its kind in the city, hence the name "Alpha." Two young men made it possible: Dr. Robert Tribbitt, a dentist, and Dr. William Method, a physician. No hospital in Columbus offered a black doctor or surgeon an opportunity to practice, and the community was in critical need of medical care. Method and Tribbitt purchased an old residence of six rooms and a bath in the heart of the largest of the African American communities in the city and later included a building next to it. The hospital, though small, had modern sterilizing and X-ray equipment. In the first thirteen weeks of the hospital's operation, it served forty-two patients, thirty-two of whom needed operations. East Long Street is a street of great historical significance to the African American community, as documented in the talks, books, and walking-tour guidebooks of the late poet and historian Anna Bishop.

The Urban Spirit Coffee Shop opened in the spring of 2008 in the rehabilitated Alpha Hospital building. The owner, Charity Martin-Via, was the recipient of a Preservation Award from the Columbus Landmarks Foundation for contributing to the revitalization of the historic East Long Street commercial district. Also contributing to the King-Lincoln-Bronzeville neighborhood's renaissance, the 1928 Lincoln Theatre (not pictured), which recently underwent a $13.5 million restoration, reopened in 2009 as a performing arts center and jazz academy. The Lincoln Theatre is listed in the National Register of Historic Places for its association with the rich cultural history of the African American community. The building, developed by an African American fraternal organization and constructed by an African American construction company, was a center for stage and screen entertainment for many decades. The interior is rich in Egyptian motif and the renovated upstairs ballroom is used for special events.

During World War II, Carl Strandlund (second from left) worked for a company that produced porcelain-enameled steel panels, a product he had patented. These panels were being manufactured for military use and for use at gas stations and hamburger stands. After the war, he sold the innovative idea of prefabricated, mass-produced single-family housing to the federal government, addressing the timely issues of a critical demand for housing for returning veterans and the surplus of vacant wartime factories. In 1947 he established the Lustron Corporation and received several multimillion-dollar loans from the Reconstruction Finance Corporation (RFC). The first Lustron houses were produced from a nine-mile assembly line in 1949 at the massive Curtiss-Wright aircraft manufacturing plant. However, the success of the company was short-lived when the U.S. Senate banking subcommittee investigated the RFC loans and recalled them in the 1950s, forcing Lustron into bankruptcy and bringing production to a halt.

In the short life span of the Lustron Corporation, approximately 2,680 Lustron houses were manufactured, and it is speculated that as many as 2,000 survive in thirty-seven states. According to a national Internet registry of Lustrons, Ohio ranks second to Illinois with more than 200 still standing, seventeen of which are in Columbus. Eight different models of homes were manufactured, varying in size, number of bedrooms, and amenities. The houses were produced in distinctive colors of blue, yellow, tan, and gray (see inset). They never needed painting, were rust- and vermin-proof, had many permanent built-ins, and, best of all for some, needed only a magnet for hanging a picture. Another of the distinctive characteristics of the houses is the zigzag porch post.

Camp Chase, shown here circa 1863, was established in 1861. Based four miles west of the statehouse, its 160 acres (from Broad Street to Sullivant Avenue) were used for training Union recruits for the Civil War. However, it soon became a war prison when captured Confederate soldiers and officers were brought north. Seriously overcrowded—at times holding more than 8,000 prisoners—at least 5,000 men died in the camp. After 1879, buildings were dismantled and the cemetery plot was deeded to the government and

fell into neglect until it was rescued in the early 1900s by a former Union veteran, William Knauss, who believed that no soldier's grave should be neglected. The remaining land reverted to farmland or was later subdivided for homes as the Hilltop (Westgate) neighborhood grew in popularity in the 1920s. In 1928 the St. Mary Magdalene Parish was founded, and work started on the present church building in 1954; construction was completed in 1956.

All that remains today of Camp Chase, the largest Confederate prisoner-of-war camp in the North, is a Confederate memorial and a cemetery for more than 2,000 bodies. St. Mary Magdalene Catholic Church on South Roys Avenue sits in a picturesque parklike setting, a symbolic representation of how the land has changed. Once part of Camp Chase, it is now an idyllic neighborhood. The Camp Chase site is listed in the National Register of Historic Places. Distinctive features of the modern church's interior include an American granite pulpit, Egyptian limestone walls, and five Carrara marble plaques and statuary. Mosaics were incorporated in 1963 and stained-glass windows date to 1966. A restored organ with more than 1,000 pipes was installed in 1990. The nearby St. Mary Magdalene School (not pictured) was staffed by the Franciscan Order of Sisters of Mary Immaculate of Joliet, Illinois, from 1929 to 1974.

Built in 1895, the old Toledo and Ohio Station has been called a cross between "a Chinese pagoda and a Moroccan bathhouse," though it is more affectionately referred to locally as "Shinto Gothic." Built by the Columbus architectural firm of Yost and Packard for use as the principal depot of the Toledo and Ohio Railroad, it was eventually used by the Hocking Valley line. Until 1955, a similar but smaller building existed on the other side of the tracks (the tracks were at grade level until 1911), and it is speculated that this was the original depot. For many years, up until its closing, it was a restaurant. Inside the present building is a large barrel-vaulted ceiling and a balcony that spans the south wall. Though the station survived floods in 1898 and 1913, it almost did not survive fire. In 1975 fire destroyed most of the interior and nearly all the roof, and it was only through the commitment of the Volunteers of America, longtime caretakers of the building since 1930, that the fire was turned into an opportunity to upgrade and renovate.

When the Volunteers of America moved their offices to another historic building across from Franklin Park, the City of Columbus purchased the building, intending to return it to public use. Three potential caretakers of the building at the time included: the Columbus Historical Society, for use as a museum; the Harley-Davidson dealership in Franklinton (the oldest in the country), for a restaurant and transportation venue; and the municipal firefighter's union, for offices and public space. It was purchased, rehabilitated,

and expanded in 2007 by the International Association of Fire Fighters Local 67 for offices and a reception hall. They took down a sizable late addition on the east side of the building, which had been used by the Volunteers of America for donations and sales, and replaced it with the architecturally compatible reception hall. The project was substantially paid for by an increase in union members' dues and volunteer labor, and is listed in the National Register of Historic Places.

Always distinctive, White Castle and its corporate headquarters have been in Columbus since 1934; the chain was founded in 1921 by Edgar Ingram and Walter Anderson in Wichita, Kansas. Concentrated mostly in the Midwest, White Castles were built on slivers of land and frequently near streetcar stops. Front Street near the river (shown here in 1929), prior to expansion of state offices, was a workingman's neighborhood with small factories and residences,

the rear facades of hotels, and department stores. "Sliders," or hamburgers with one ounce of ground meat with onions and a pickle, were affordable at five for ten cents with a coupon. White Castles started in small buildings of white brick ("white" for cleanliness, "castle" for permanence) and evolved into enamel-paneled structures. Hundreds of restaurants are still owned by the Ingram family today.

Columbus's first White Castle lasted less than two years to make way for the Ohio Departments of State Building. When the statehouse and its annex were outgrown, this 1933 building was the first of several built for state offices in the capital. A natural gas explosion in 1932 caused such damage to the nearly completed building that the facade needed to be rebuilt. The Art Moderne building displays Ohio symbolism throughout, and its white marble exterior with stylized carvings contrasts with the elaborate Art Deco ornamentation inside.

Interior features include an extensive use of marble, decorative metalwork and light fixtures, wood paneling, bronze bas reliefs, and brilliantly colored mosaics and murals. The building was rehabilitated between 2001 and 2004 as the Ohio Judicial Center, home of Ohio's supreme court and an education center open to the public. The building is listed in the National Register of Historic Places and the Columbus Register of Historic Properties, and received the James B. Recchie Design Award from the Columbus Landmarks Foundation.

By the 1910s, the elite who once populated the East Park Addition, made up of three elliptical parks and elegant homes, began to move farther out as the downtown expanded. The larger homes they had built were being leased or sold to a less affluent population. Between 1913 and 1917, 77 Jefferson Avenue was rented to a middle-class family of five, two parents and three boys. The middle boy, James Thurber, became one of the most notable American humorists of the twentieth century. It was while living here during his developmental years that many of his talents as an author, humorist, and cartoonist were nurtured. He took classes at the Ohio State University as a "townie" still living at home. Although he never completed his degree, he began reporting for the *Columbus Dispatch* in 1920, worked for the *New Yorker* in 1927, and began publishing cartoons for the magazine in 1930. In spite of failing eyesight, Thurber wrote nearly forty books before he died in 1961.

The Thurber House, once in dilapidated condition, was rehabilitated in 1984 and became the home of a nonprofit literary center and museum of Thurber's materials. The interior decor of the house reflects the time period during which Thurber resided in the house with his family. References to these years are included in his autobiography, *My Life and Hard Times*, and the play *A Thurber Carnival*. At the request of the Thurber family, the house is a "living museum," where visitors are encouraged to touch the Thurber memorabilia that is displayed throughout the house. The former dining room serves as a museum shop and the third floor has been turned into an apartment for visiting writers and artists. The Thurber House is listed in the National Register of Historic Places and the Columbus Register of Historic Properties.

In 1899 William Fish, whose family mansion stood diagonally across the street from the north entrance to Goodale Park on Dennison Avenue, donated the pagoda gate. The Fish family owned and operated stone and pressed brick companies, and they were the first American manufacturers of brick made from slate or shale. The faces carved into the pillars depict the seven ages of man from Shakespeare's play *As You Like It*. Goodale Park originated in 1851, when Dr. Lincoln Goodale gave forty acres of pristine land at the northern boundary of the city to Columbus for use as the city's first park. During the Civil War, the park became Camp Jackson. Goodale had come in 1805 to Franklinton, the pioneer settlement on the west side of the Scioto River. As a young doctor, he invested in large pieces of property on the east side of the river. After the War of 1812, when the capital had been established on the east side of the Scioto, Goodale's holdings became profitable and made his gift possible.

Goodale Park and the adjacent Victorian Village neighborhood are nurtured by several active volunteer-based organizations. The Friends of Goodale Park is a nonprofit organization formed in 1987, recognizing that the surrounding neighborhood needed to take greater responsibility to keep this bucolic urban park. Projects they have undertaken include a major tree-planting initiative and the construction of a gazebo and expanded shelter house. The Victorian Village Society is a nonprofit civic association focused on building a stronger community for the village and neighborhoods in the Short North area. The society has been responsible for renovation and improvements to the Goodale Park caretaker's residence, and for the addition of new signage and bike racks for the park. The Victorian Village Commission is an agency of the city government established in 1973 by the Columbus City Council. The commission is the first line of approval for all exterior improvements and repairs done to any property in the historic district.

The Buckeye Steel Castings Company plant was itself made of structural steel by the American Bridge Company. Steam power and direct-current electricity drove the machinery that made steel castings for railroad cars. The area around the factory—Steelton—was named for the product. Even the neighborhood bank on South Parsons Avenue was named the Steelton branch. The steel industry debuted in 1904, but the roots of Buckeye Steel stretched back fifty years to other businesses: a malleable iron company that almost went bankrupt and a small iron foundry that served the agricultural needs of the local farmers. Also known as the Steelton Works of the Carnegie Steel Company or the Columbus Steel Works and Buckeye Malleable Iron Company, Buckeye Steel succeeded for a simple reason. By the early twentieth century, railroad couplers were required by federal law. As American railroads grew, so did a need for the couplers. From 1908 to 1928, Samuel Prescott Bush, great-grandfather of former U.S. president George W. Bush, was company president.

In 1967 the parent company of Buckeye Steel, Buckeye International Inc., was formed; it was then acquired by Worthington Industries through a stock merger. Worthington sold Buckeye Steel in 1999. The Columbus Steel Castings Company was formed in 2003, created out of the assets of Buckeye Steel, which filed for bankruptcy in 2002. Today, Columbus Steel makes large steel components for railway freight cars and large machinery, and continues to operate out of this former Buckeye Steel foundry that has been in use for more than a century on the South Side. The foundry covers an area of more than ninety acres, twenty-two of which are under roofs. As such, it is the largest single-site steel foundry in North America.

Children stand at the corner of City Park Avenue and Lansing (Bismarck prior to World War I) Street; the photographer is looking north in the neighborhood known as the South End. In 1898, when this photo was taken, most inhabitants of these houses might already be second-generation German Americans. Germans began to arrive in Columbus in such numbers from the 1830s to 1870s that, by the century's end, it was estimated that one in four Columbus inhabitants was German or of German descent. Small single-story cottages were becoming a popular architectural form and had first appeared in New Orleans, whose free black population borrowed them from Haitians who remembered them from West Africa. It was an architectural style that traveled by way of the Mississippi River, like jazz would forty years later, making Columbus one of the northernmost points of "shotgun" architecture—a name that had nothing to do with firing shotguns but was a corruption of a West African word meaning "house."

Years after World War I ended, the name changes in the South End that were prompted by anti-German hysteria were reversed. Schiller Park lost its World War I name, Washington Park; however, the former Schiller Avenue kept its new name, Whittier Avenue. The South End name remained, but a newly named section, German Village, became Columbus's first historic district in 1963 by an act of the city council. The German Village Commission was the city's first architectural review board, also established in 1963. German Village was listed in the National Register of Historic Places in 1974 and the boundaries were expanded in 1980. More than 1,600 buildings have been renovated in this neighborhood since 1960. The German Village Society is a membership-supported nonprofit organization that serves as caretakers of the village, and is presently made up of more than 1,000 committed preservationists. The neighborhood of German Village was designated as a Preserve America Community by the White House in 2007.

The old Ohio Field on North High Street, with a seating capacity of 6,100, was not able to accommodate all those who attended football games. Dr. Thomas French and Director of Athletics Lynn W. St. John were instrumental in planning and especially financing a stadium that many thought would be impossible to fill with a capacity of 30,000 seats. Citywide parades and pageants raised expectations that a new stadium could be financed. Ohio State's invitation to the Rose Bowl in 1921 helped cement the deal. Architect Howard Dwight Smith built a 66,210-seat stadium at a cost of about $1.5 million, only $82,500 over budget. The elegant and unique double-decked, horseshoe-shaped structure with an open end won Smith the top award for excellence in public works from the American Institute of Architects.

Ohio Stadium, now listed in the National Register of Historic Places, is a nationally recognized college athletic facility. Greatly expanded and renovated between 1999 and 2001, the stadium, affectionately known as "the Shoe," now has the capacity to seat 102,329 spectators. The renovation greatly altered the exterior and the interior. Lost were the egalitarian nature of the all-weather seats, a sense of the original design, and the track on which Ohio State student and Olympian Jesse Owens practiced in the 1930s. Gained were skyboxes and press boxes, a massive electronic scoreboard, and more ladies' restrooms. One of the two south-end towers that were retained in the expansion is evident in the photo. The Victory Bell, rung after every winning game since 1954, is housed in the southeast tower. More than thirty-six million fans have attended games in the venue since its opening game in October 1922.

The Ohio State Archaeological and Historical Society incorporated in 1885, and its first museum was built at the entrance to the Ohio State University in 1924 at Fifteenth Avenue and North High Street. Both the university and the historical society were brought into being by the enormous support of pioneer Lucas Sullivant's sons. In addition to being a library with more than a million manuscripts and documents (not including newspapers, maps, and books), the museum contained three floors of exhibits from the prehistoric Mound Builders to pioneer tools and farm equipment, a hall of paintings, an original furnished log cabin, and the requisite stuffed animals and birds. In addition, near the auditorium was a World War I memorial rotunda with bronze reliefs depicting scenes from the war.

Today, Sullivant Hall contains the Ohio State University's Undergraduate Student Library, the intimate Sullivant Theater, and the Music and Dance Library. Its prominent location, once the heart of the commercial district and gateway to the university, is in transition due to the relocation of the Long's Bookstore and the new South Campus Gateway redevelopment five blocks south on North High. The "Victorious Doughboy" statue that once stood in front of Sullivant Hall and purportedly winked at the many "pure" coeds passing by was moved to the front lawn of the new Ohio Historical Center at Interstate 71 and Seventeenth Avenue, when it opened as the new home of the Ohio Historical Society in 1970. The sculptor, Bruce Wilder Saville, was a professor at the Ohio State University and cast the piece in 1924 to honor veterans of World War I. Saville sculpted multiple war memorials around the country.

Though football had been at the university since 1879, there appears to have been no formally organized Ohio State student football team until 1887, when students played the Columbus Buggy Company team. Ohio Field, built in 1908, was the university's first official athletic field, located approximately where Arps Hall, 1945 North High Street, the parking garage, and Ramseyer Hall are located today. High Street is behind the grandstand, and the neighborhood houses (now gone) on West Woodruff Avenue form a boundary for Ohio Field. The stadium had a seating capacity of only 6,100 and sometimes drew 14,000 fans, which caused traffic jams and resulted in hundreds being turned away on game days. The fans were drawn here to see the phenomenal athletic skills of Columbus-born Ohio State student Charles "Chic" Harley, who was a three-time all-American (1916, 1917, 1919). The inset photo shows crowds in front of the ticket gates in 1909.

Ohio Field's brick gateways and stands for the fans were removed in 1924, and today many of those who drive, bike, skateboard, jog, or stroll past this area have no idea that this indentation in the grassy lawn was once the hub of the Ohio State University's football activity. The site is memorialized by a small historic marker near North High Street. Among the storefronts on the east side of North High Street, Chic Harley is enshrined in a terra-cotta storefront on the old University Theater, appearing to be leaping over the awning of a restaurant. On the north side of the former Ohio Field, Ramseyer Hall was built in 1932. Serving as the College of Education's learning laboratory and progressive University School for thirty-seven years until 1967, Ramseyer Hall is now the home of the university's Art Education Department, School of Educational Policy and Leadership, and School of Teaching and Learning. Arps Hall was built on the south side of the former field in 1925.

At the north end of the campus's central area, known as the Oval, Hayes Hall was named for ex-president Rutherford B. Hayes, who died a month after the building opened in December 1892. Constructed to house the departments of manual, domestic, and technical training, it was the first Ohio college building used exclusively for this instruction. Though Hayes Hall is often listed as the work of the partnership of Columbus architects Frank Yost and J. W. Packard, who were designing Orton Hall at the same time, Packard was the sole designer of this Romanesque Revival building. Hayes Hall is said to be the oldest building on campus; however, technically, the central power plant for the university had to be completed and put into operation before Hayes could be opened, so the power plant is thus the oldest. The Armory (right and inset) also was done by Yost and Packard; it opened in 1898 and served, over the years, as a naval armory and drill hall, as well as a public auditorium space.

Hayes Hall is listed in the National Register of Historic Places. Though the building has been greatly altered in the rear, the front facade is virtually unchanged, including its massive arched entry of brown sandstone and the use of multiple materials, including contrasting rock-faced sandstone and redbrick walls. The university's Department of History of Art is currently housed in Hayes Hall. Though the Armory, which had been a distinctive landmark for many years, burned in 1958, the adjacent Mershon Auditorium survived. In 1989 Mershon's new neighbor was the Wexner Center for the Visual Arts (see inset), built on the site of the former Armory. The Wexner Center references the former Armory in its castlelike design. Richard Trott and Partners of Columbus and Eisenman Robertson of New York City were the original Wexner architects, selected through an international design competition. The Wexner Center for the Visual Arts was renovated in 2005.

Built in 1891–93 by the highly creative Columbus architectural firm of Yost and Packard, Orton Hall was built to honor Dr. Edward Orton Sr. as both the first university president (1873–81, when it was known as the Ohio Agricultural and Mechanical College) and as the first state geologist of Ohio. The building's Richardsonian Romanesque–style exterior is a lesson in geology, constructed of forty different kinds of Ohio stone arranged in stratigraphic order as found in nature and culminating in extinct animals as gargoyles around the top of the tower. The building's geology museum was intended to be the university's first semipermanent library until a larger facility could be built. Before 1934, the original red-tile roof and the skylights were replaced. In World War I, the skylights had been frequent victims to the "wooden" bombs dropped by the university's fledgling aero squadron, which used the Oval for target practice. The inset shows Orton Hall under construction in 1893; the main image captures a photography class in progress from 1908.

Listed in the National Register of Historic Places, Orton Hall is home to the Orton Memorial Library of Geology, the Orton Geological Museum, the Department of Geology and Mineralogy, and the laboratories of the Departments of Paleontology, Historical Geology, and Sedimentology. The building's geology lesson continues inside in the vestibule, where there are twenty-four columns, each made of a different variety of Ohio stone, with capitals carved with geological symbols; the floor tiles are made from Ohio clay. The Orton Memorial Library of Geology, housed since 1924 in the room with a balcony, is the second-largest academic geosciences library in the country, with more than 112,000 volumes and 200,000 maps. The original architecture is complemented by art from the personal collection of Dr. Edward Orton Jr. On display in the Orton Geological Museum are a giant sloth skeleton; Ohio minerals, rocks, and fossils; a fluorescent mineral booth; and mastodon molars. Outside, a glacial boulder was taken from the Iuka Ravine and "planted" in honor of Dr. Edward Orton Sr.

The Ohio Union opened in 1911 in an elegant Jacobethan Revival–style building—but without furnishings. Apparently, no money had been set aside for furniture, and a committee was put into place to find a way to furnish the building through donations. The interior, however, was rich with touches found in any fine home of the era: alcoves, fireplaces, and rich wood paneling. It is one of the oldest student union buildings in the country, built as the result of a student-led campaign to provide a safe center exclusively for student use and as an alternative to "urban vices." The building went by a number of names: Students' Building, Club House, Student Union, and in 1919, it was also called the Ohio Union Mess Hall because a temporary kitchen and dining room were added for the nearby School of Military Aeronautics. In the 1930s, Olympic gold medalist Jesse Owens ate here almost every day because no establishment on High Street would serve him. In the 1950s, the building was the home of Student Health Services.

Once threatened with demolition, the original Ohio Union was renovated in 1985. It is one of the four buildings on the Ohio State University campus listed in the National Register of Historic Places. Student Health Services moved from the building in 1969. Most of the remaining student services have moved to other locations on campus. Named for former university president Harold L. Enarson in 1986, the building now houses the offices for Undergraduate Admissions and the First Year Experience Program, the Arts and Sciences Honors Program, and the Scholars Program. The James J. Mager Student Visitor Center, housed in the 1996 addition at the west end of the building, is a valuable resource for all prospective students and serves approximately 30,000 visitors a year. This center will relocate to the new student union that is currently under construction. Enarson Hall retains much of its historic integrity in spite of having had seven additions to its original structure.

For years, the front door of the Ohio State University at Fifteenth Avenue and North High Street was acknowledged but not defined. By 1944 students, professors, visitors, and football fans moved freely through the newly built Graduates' Gateway, also known as the Alumni Gateway. The impressive pillars and curved stone benches were gifts from the graduating classes of 1931, 1938, 1939, and 1941. The president's house, barely seen to the right, was the 1856 Joseph Strickler house, which predated the university but housed five presidents, the last in 1938. The house would be replaced by the Mershon Auditorium within a decade of this picture. On the left, the old Ohio State Archaeological and Historical Society Building (now Sullivant Hall) had already been operating as a museum for three decades.

Historically, the intersection of Fifteenth Avenue and North High Street was the site of pregame football bonfires, the beginning of fraternity and sorority row, and the site of the largest student bookstore in the United States, Long's Bookstore (now closed). The path from the Main Library across the Oval to High Street and into the neighborhood was known as "the Long Walk." Security concerns in the 1960s and 1970s ended vehicular traffic through the entrance. In the 1960s, students protested against the city police arresting people for jaywalking, and also against the university's ban on free speech. Disturbances resulting from drug arrests on High Street were common. The heightened unrest of May 1970 shut down the university. Massive student protests over the Vietnam War and the State of Ohio's actions at Kent State University (which led to the shooting deaths of students) closed the symbolic open Alumni Gateway. When the Wexner Center for the Visual Arts opened in the 1980s, the Long Walk terminated in a landscaped pedestrian mall.

# INDEX